AUTOGENICS 3.0

THE NEW WAY TO MINDFULNESS AND MEDITATION

Second Edition Revised

Luis de Rivera, MD

MADRID * MONTREAL

ICAT Information Center
Institute of Psychotherapy and Psychosomatic Research
Avenida de Filipinas 52, 8B 28003 Madrid, Spain.
Phone: +34 91 534 2941; e-mail: info@psicoter.es

Interior design and figures by
Helena Hernandez, Justin de Rivera
Leonor de Rivera, Luis Hernandez.

Library of Congress Cataloging-in-Publication Data in process

LCCN assignment pending

ISBN-13: 978-1548162054
ISBN-10: 1548162051

Printed in the United States of America in acid-free paper

Also by Luis de Rivera, MD:

- *Psychodynamics of Mobbing*
- *A Unified Theory of Work Place Harassment*
- *Psicoterapia Autogena*
- *Crisis Emocionales*
- *Sindromes de Estres*
- *El Maltrato Psicologico*
- *Medicina Psicosomatica*
- *Psiconeuroendocrinologia*
- *Las Claves del Mobbing*
- *El Test de Memoria por Ordenador*
- *Manual de Psiquiatria*
- *El Metodo Epidemiologico en Salud Mental*
- *Adaptación Española del SCL90R – (Pearson)*
- *LSB 50. Listado de Síntomas Breve*
- *LIPT 60. Cuestionario de Acoso Laboral*

Follow the author: @luisderivera

CONTENTS

1.

INTRODUCTION

"Meditation" and "Mindfulness," two words practically unknown in the Western world until the late sixties, are now the name of exploding trends. The rare honor of two *Time* magazine covers has been dedicated to them in this millennium,[1] first to meditation in 2003 and then to mindfulness in 2014. Millions of people are going into meditation, and thousands of centers are opening all over the world to teach the techniques. Doctors are recommending meditation to their patients and psychologists are including mindfulness in their psychotherapies, some of them convinced that they are jumping into a most recent revolutionary discovery.

The truth is that those mind-training methods have been around for more than five thousand years and have been discovered and rediscovered many times in different parts of the world.

What is going on now? What is bringing to us this recent upsurge of a millenary Far East tradition? Is it all a passing fad? Are we entering a new age of enlightenment? Are we just tired of materialistic pursuits and looking for a new inner world? So many questions…but let me ask you the only important one:

What is making you read this book right now?

Perhaps you are just curious, or maybe you are looking for serious instruction. This may be your first approach to meditation, or perhaps you have been faltering across many and variegated schools. Maybe you are an expert meditator, or perhaps you are still trying to convince yourself that you can do it.

Sure, you hear about the mighty healthy effects of mindfulness; perhaps you are interested in the development of your inner self. Maybe you feel attracted to a doctrine that promises spiritual happiness in this very life. All those reasons are sound reasons; those were the reasons that led me to yoga, to meditation, and to autogenics when I was in my teens.

Whatever your reasons are, I am here with you. After a lifelong practice, I am ready to share with you everything that I have learned. All that is in this book I have tried, not only in myself but also in thousands of persons who came to me, some for help on their symptoms and sufferings, some for professional instruction, but all to find a new way of living their lives. There is much more than "relaxation" in what you are going to learn.

What Do Meditation and Mindfulness Mean?

The human experience of mindfulness and meditation exists, but it is hard to put into words. Some authors use the words "meditation" and "mindfulness" interchangeably to translate the Buddhist word *sati*,[2] whereas others use them to bring another technical term, s*hamata*.[3] In truth, *sati* and *shamata* are untranslatable words, because the experience they denote does not exist in the Western culture. This may explain the current terminological confusion, in which the same name applies to different experiences, the same experience receives different names, and the same word designates a mental state and the technique to achieve this state.

Communicating the experience to you is more important that scholar-linguistic disquisitions, but some definitions are necessary. As a technical term, I recommend defining *meditation* as a mental activity, different from reasoning and imagination, which develops with specific training and produces effects that can be described and compared objectively. The practice of meditation consists of keeping sustained attention on an object, image, sound, concept, or experience, without expecting any particular result.

This special way of concentrating attention, without purpose or finality, is what defines meditation, differentiating it from other mental activities. *Mindfulness* is the attentional state that develops with meditation and also the particular way of using attention in meditation. Meditation training is thus training in mindfulness.

You may find mindfulness defined in different texts as total awareness, as completely open perception, as "been in the here and now," and so on. This refers to an attitude of mind characterized by openness to experience and renouncing to all critique or judgment. To complicate matters further, you may also find opposite definitions of mindfulness, like "absorption in a particular stimulus with disregard of the rest" and, conversely, as "global perception of all stimuli without undue attention to any single one."

Regardless of the words used, you must know that all those states, activities, and experiences exist, even if the English language lacks appropriate names for most of them. That is why you would find the same word applied to various experiences and the same experience referred to by different words. Do not worry; I will help you to make sense out of this confusion along the book, it's easy.

What is autogenics?

The history of autogenics[4] begins in the 1920's, when the German physician, Dr. Johannes Schultz, was experimenting with the psychophysiological effects of autohypnosis. The method he described, autogenic training, proved to be very beneficial for the relaxation of body and mind and became a standard tool in German psychosomatic medicine, where it remains active today. This early phase, considered by many a form of self-hypnotic relaxation, is what I call Autogenics 1.0. Schultz tried at some point to establish the differences between autogenic training and autohypnosis, introducing the concept of "passive concentration," which was further elaborated by Luthe.

The next serious breakthrough, which I call Autogenics 2.0, came in 1961, when a German-Canadian pupil of Schultz, Wolfgang Luthe, discovered that the unpleasant phenomena which appear at times during the practice of autogenic training were not just undesirable side effects but the expression of a therapeutic process.

Luthe described and classified the "training symptoms" under the name of "autogenic discharges" and demonstrated that they were related to the traumatic history of the patient. Luthe considered the autogenic discharges as the expression of a natural process of "autogenic neutralization," the dissolution and liberation of the pathogenic effect of past traumatic events.

By his theory of the therapeutic value of autogenic discharges, Luthe developed clinical methods to facilitate autogenic neutralization.[5] Working with Luthe, I realized that his method of autogenic abreaction was tackling the same mental processes as Freud's psychoanalysis,[6] and in due time, I was able to develop a combined approach, appropriately termed "autogenic analysis."

In the early seventies, working with Raymond Prince in the Montreal Mental Hygiene Institute, I was treating university students who had gone through a bad psychedelic trip. This gave me firsthand opportunity to study the relationship between drugs, states of consciousness, and meditation. Most of my psychedelic patients went back to their normal lives without much difficulty, although some slipped into a more or less chronic mental disorder. But, what deeply impressed me, was a small third group who experienced lasting improvements in their mental balance and creativity. Treatment with autogenics seemed to facilitate the good outcomes and showed serious potential to prevent further drug misuse.[7]

Some of my students pointed to me that TM, or Transcendental Meditation, a simplified Western adaptation of old yoga practices, produced similar results in drug addicts than those obtained by autogenic training. Curious and eager for knowledge as I was, I got personal experience with Transcendental Meditation and realized that the subjective experience was very similar to that produced by autogenics. I also tried other methods, such as Silva mind control, tai chi, yoga, and *vipassana*, much to the same conclusion.

At the time, I was also influenced by the work of Claudio Naranjo on the psychology of meditation[8] and by the description of the "relaxation response" by Herbert Benson,[9] two works that marked a "before and after" on my consideration of the altered states of consciousness as a scientific endeavor.

All this eclectic experience got me convinced that the different methods were just diverse ways of training the same capacity to self-induce amplified states of consciousness. To avoid the negative connotations of the word "altered" as in "altered states of consciousness" (ASC), I changed early in my work "altered" by "amplified," proposing the expression "amplified states of consciousness" to denominate those special mental states to which meditation leads.[10]

To test my theory, with the invaluable collaboration of Dra. Reyes Trujillo, we conducted an extensive comparative study on the psychological effects of different meditation methods.[11] By and large, we demonstrated that the subjective phenomena produced or perceived on those states were substantially similar. The most significant differences were related to the experience of the meditator, regarding years and frequency of practice, rather than to the technique applied.

In an international meeting of psychotherapy in Switzerland, our research group suggested the general umbrella name of "Amplified States of Consciousness Induction Therapies" (ASCI Therapies,[12] for short) to facilitate comparative studies of the increasing number of therapies using meditation methods.

In Autogenics 3.0 there is a definite shift from autohypnosis to meditation. The autogenic exercises are no longer considered "auto hypnotic" as in Autogenics 1.0 but "meditative." This means that it is no longer a question of autosuggestion of a given sensation but of passive concentration on that sensation, actually present in the part of the body under consideration. Other significant innovations of Autogenics 3.0 are the new method of "feeling meditation" and the evolution of the classic technique of psychological autogenic modification in the new method of autogenic reconstruction.

Version	Method	Purpose	Author
1.0 Autogenic Training	Autohypnosis Passive concentration	Relaxation	Schultz
2.0 Autogenic Therapy	Passive acceptance	Neutralization	Luthe
3.0 Autogenics	Meditation	Self-development	de Rivera

In conclusion, nothing is conflicting between autogenics, yoga, *vipassana*, and other forms of serious meditation. We are all working on the same human nature, training the same mental functions, activating the same parts of the brain. Autogenics 3.0 offers the most efficient, complete, and safe way for Western practitioners. Most other approaches try to adapt ancient Far-East religious practices to Western needs and mentality, whereas autogenics grew inside of the European scientific tradition, out of an early-twentieth-century medical approach for the treatment of psychosomatic disorders. Ever since, the development of autogenics has followed the pragmatic way of balancing experimentation and observation—much in the Western scientific tradition—with the training of mental faculties under the guidance of a recognized master—much in the Eastern introspective tradition.

So wrote to me a distinguished meditation teacher:

Dear Luis, the way you work with attention has facilitated my meditative process. Your teachings have improved the amplitude and quality of my mindful state, and the attention to the present moment becomes easier. Autogenics has also given me a new tool for stress reduction and for anxiety management with my clients.

Santos Martin, the Transpersonal Mindfulness Institute, Canarias

2.

WHO INVENTED MEDITATION?

By oral tradition and ancient religious texts, we know that this way of training attention is at least five thousand years old. We do not know who or how initiated this practice, but I would say that is an achievement more important to human evolution that the discovery of the wheel. I think that meditative states are at the origin of all religions and that the persons gifted with easy access to amplified states of consciousness were the first leaders of humankind.

Meditation is a way of training attention, so let us first see how untrained attention works. Natural attention is like a radar, ready to detect any changes in the environment. This radar quality has high survival value, because anything that shifts in a safe environment may indicate the presence of a dangerous agent. Let us imagine our primitive ancestor, or any animal for that matter, relaxing calmly in the middle of the forest and then getting aroused briskly at the breaking of a small twig. His attention will be drawn to the noise; he will inspect the surroundings attentively, searching where the sound came from and what produced it, all this accompanied by the increased physiological activity needed to fight or to flight. This concentrated attention has the definite finality of spotting and avoiding a dangerous threat, and our ancestor will keep it for as long as it takes to feel safe again.

The radar function of attention gets also activated by anything interesting, such as a beautiful being or an appetizing food. Danger and attraction are the two primary triggers of natural attention. You can easily observe this phenomenon in contemporary domestic animals: When nothing exciting or threatening is happening around, your pet will fall comfortably asleep. In humans it is harder to see this principle in action; we have a very active world inside our heads and not only disturbing changes in the environment keep us awake but also and foremost the internal turmoil of our minds.

It is tough to sustain attention on an unchanging or uninteresting stimulus for more than a few seconds.[13] If your ancestress were to be confronted with a wild animal when neither fight nor flight would be possible, she is likely to remain immobile, as she knows by instinct that the smallest movement—change—will attract the beast attention to her.

Sustaining attention in unchanging or uninteresting stimuli is not natural but can be achieved with appropriate training. We all learned to do it first thing in school when our teachers forced us to pay attention to their boring explanations. In autogenics, we call this kind of sustained attention "active concentration," meaning that you pay attention to achieve some particular result, in this case learning the lesson and being praised by the teacher. It is the same concentration we apply to arithmetic calculations or to accomplish any ordinary task.

Going back to our imaginary exploration of prehistoric times, and drawing also from personal experience, I can imagine a primitive man gazing at the sea or at the waving leaves of a forest and getting slowly into a most pleasurable state of mind. This had happened to me, long before I had any instruction on meditative techniques, so I am sure it has happened to many people, including our ancestors and probably to you. Please, remember if you ever had this experience, if you ever felt relaxed and peaceful just by gazing at the sea, at the clouds, at the fire, or at something similar.

As it probably did happen with fire, our ancestors may have discovered mindfulness by chance. Then, as they did with fire, they were able, little by little, to implement the necessary steps to produce the mindful state at will. Let us imagine a small band of ancestors, sitting around a fire in the middle of the night with nothing better to do than getting absorbed in the fluid movement of the flames. Some may have fallen asleep, while others entered an alternative reality in which they would experience strange phenomena. This might well have been our first departure from the concrete physical animal world in the symbolic human-mental world.

Fire was considered holy and associated with divinity probably because it came from heaven, like lightning falling in a tree, but I prefer to think that the fascination induced by fire is at the root of a collective state of worship that evolved into religions. I fancy that the first Buddhist monastery was born by chance around a prehistoric bonfire, long before Siddhartha Gautama was born. After this, it was only a question of getting organized and inventing new methods to produce the live-experience at will.[14]

For millennia, the workings of managed attention were left to naturally gifted individuals, who often claimed to be in contact with deities and other supernatural beings. Some of them must have been right, as all the great religions were founded by notorious experiencers of amplified states of consciousness. In an earthlier plane, it seems that many scientific discoveries have been made on those amplified states.[15] At some point, the procedures to get into the amplified states of consciousness were understood well enough to be described and taught. The feelings of fusion with a transcendental entity, a well-recognized effect of meditation, can be induced by some practices common to all religions.

Yoga, the oldest organized method of meditation, is not really a religion, although it effortlessly merged with Indian Hinduism and with the Tibetan Bon religion. Schutlz (1932) considers that "autogenic training may be described as psychophysiologically rationalized and systematized yoga." The transmission of the early yoga practices and philosophy relied on oral tradition for millennia; their earliest written records are the Vedas (about 1700 BC) and the Bhagavad Gita (about 500 BC). The yoga sutras of Patanjali (200 BC) are a collection of 196 aphorisms with practical psychological instructions still followed today.[16]

Buddha, despite widespread popular belief, was a late newcomer to meditation. As a runaway prince, known as Siddhartha Gautama Sakyamuni, he trained for many years with various yoga masters until he became a full expert in *shamata*. Still unsatisfied, he continued his own path, created *vipassana*, his special brand of meditation, and achieved full understanding of infinite reality in 530 BC. In commemoration of this event, he changed his name to Buddha, which means "the one that has awakened" in the Pali language. He summarized his doctrine in the Four Noble Truths and the Noble Eightfold Path. Numbering was important in early Buddhism, probably as an aid in the memorization of the teachings, learned by heart and transmitted orally. In the first century BC, some monks began writing parts of the doctrine, but it was not until the fifth century AD that Buddhaghosa wrote the first comprehensive treatise.[17] Of the eight noble paths, the last three contain precise practical instructions on meditation technique, being the rest concerned with the philosophical theory and the moral instructions preparatory for the experience.[18]

While Buddha was creating his school in India, Lao-Tse was working out the doctrine of the tao in China. The philosophical principles of Taoism are oneness, dynamic balance, and harmonious action. The physical practices of Taoism, like tai chi, rightly called "moving meditation," follow those principles and are quite different from the immobility of the yoga asanas. Taoism and Buddhism merged to create Chinese meditation or *Ch'an,* which moved to Japan and evolved into Zen. The ethics of Japanese martial arts or *Budo* are a way to liberate the ego and to achieve the live-experience of unity. In the Zen art of archery, for instance, "the archer, the arrow and the target are one." With this mentality, there is no way you can fail.[19]

Again, at the same time, about 500 BC, the Greek philosophers who set in motion the Western mindset were also heavily concerned with the liberation of suffering. It is intriguing that in this period of human history, never repeated, several separate cultures achieved similar solutions for the same essential human problem.[20] The Greeks did not found anything close to religion, much to the contrary; they were quite against the simple religions of their time. Neither did they develop any particular meditation technique but discovered *Biotechne,* literally, the technique of living, or art of life, the philosophical way to achieve happiness.[21]

Jewish meditation begins around 500 BC (again!) with the Merkabah mystical practices of the prophets, centered on the Ezequiel chariot vision and the Talmudic accounts of the Genesis. Jewish orthodoxy warned against Merkabah mysterious practices (that is why they remained mysterious). In the thirteenth century, there was a strong revival of Jewish mysticism, with the Kabala and the meditation on the letters of the Jewish alphabet.[22] The Essenes were another group of Jewish mystics, active since 200 BC. Very secretive in their time, they became famous in last century, after their writings, lost for millennia, were discovered in the *Dead Sea Scrolls*. The similitude of the doctrine contained on the *Dead Sea Scrolls* with that contained in the Evangels led to suspicion that Jesus of Nazareth studied with the Essenes during the twenty years he was lost from public life.

Christian mysticism originated with the desert fathers around the second century AD. They left profuse writings of their experiences, collected in *The Philokalia.*[23] Their best-known meditation is the Pray of the Heart, still in wide usage among devout Christians.[24] Middle-Ages Spain produced great Christian mystics, such as Juan de la Cruz and Teresa de Jesus, who wrote a fascinating treatise of her experiences, the *Castillo Interior* (The Interior Castle), which has some surprising similitudes with the descriptions of the seven Jhanas.[25] The order of Cistercians keep those practices alive in their monasteries, and Thomas Merton has made them accessible to the public.[26] From a different perspective, the Jesuit Tony de Mello has elaborated an impressive integration of Christian and Buddhist practices.[27]

Islamic meditation began shortly after the preaching of the prophet with the *Dhikr*, mantric-like repetition of Koranic *suras*. Another approach is Sufism, periodically persecuted, like Jewish and Christian mysticism, because the inclination of their adepts to criticize official religious leaders. The basic Sufi meditations are the concentration on divine love, on music and whirling dancing, and on esoteric tales that require transcending ordinary reasoning to be understood. Some followers of Sufis, known as fakirs, renounce all material attachments, including the nourishing and care of their own body, an extreme form of spiritual devotion not unknown to other esoteric religious traditions. Despite the strong roots of Sufism in Islam, some scholars date its origins to pre-Islamic times, with common roots in the Essenes, the Pythagorean mystics, and the Zoroastrians.[28]

As you see, the discovery of meditation has taken place many times in many different places. Its common association with religion is easy to understand because meditation often induces the experience of transcendence in predisposed individuals. Nowadays, meditation also gained a large following because of the beneficial psychological effects of its regular practice, much more so in the current craze about health and fitness. Meditation is nowadays widely accepted as a therapeutic tool and even more as an aid to professional and business success.[29] Still, some masters complain about the applied approaches to meditation—which they call "materialistic spirituality"—insisting that the real aim of meditation is neither personal gain nor serving religious creeds, but discovering the inner eternal being.[30]

The Fourth Way, the spiritual school initiated by the Armenian mystic Gurdjieff in the nineteenth century and continued by Ouspensky and others,[31] follows the principle of personal evolution, renouncing to all religious beliefs and materialistic gains. The Fourth Way toward higher human awareness purports to be a superior synthesis of all three previous ways, those of the yogi, the monk, and the fakir (hence the name of "Fourth Way"). The Fourth Way parts from the principle that ordinary humans are asleep to higher consciousness, as sleeping people are asleep to the usual waking state. The aim of the work is awakening to this higher consciousness, thus producing a different kind of human being.[32]

On general review, when approaching one of the myriad meditation schools available in present times, you are to consider three fundamental aspects: (1) the philosophy or beliefs underlying the teachings of the school, (2) the moral or ethical instructions recommended to its practitioners, and (3) the procedure to induce the mindful state.

This book concentrates on the technical aspects of meditation and is devoid of moral and philosophical considerations, not because those issues are not important, but because autogenics has developed from scientific inquiry and from therapeutic practice, not from religious or philosophical studies.

On the other hand, I have observed that a loving understanding of nature and of fellow humans develops gradually with the regular practice of autogenics.[33] Ethical behavior is the inevitable outcome of optimal physiological self-regulation, well-balanced psychological dynamics, and empathic socialization. Rather than asking adherence to a set of precepts, I recommend the regular practice of autogenics, to secure the unfolding of your natural ability to become yourself entirely.

The technical information presented in the following chapters is useful for practitioners of other methods of meditation. Basic autogenics is the easiest and most efficient way to develop passive concentration and passive acceptance, the two mind functions required for *shamata* and *vipassana* meditation. Many students of mindfulness have confirmed this observation and benefited from autogenics to improve their regular technique.

The primary method of autogenics is somatosensory meditation, also referred to as "basic training" or "basic autogenics." Learning and practicing the advanced methods require mastery of the basic autogenic training.

Advanced autogenics activates the same natural mind-brain processes that basic autogenics, only in a more powerful and efficient way. Before they are attempted, a strong period of basic training is required.

The advanced methods of autogenics are:

- Feeling meditation, which specifically improves the limbic capacity to process emotions into feelings and then transforms feelings into worthy information.

- Autogenic analysis: an evolution of autogenic abreaction.

- Autogenic modification, a useful remnant of the autohypnotic past of autogenics.

- Autogenic reconstruction, clinical application of integrative transformative psychotherapy.

AUTOGENIC METHODS AND MEDITATION

Meditation	Autogenic method
Static focus	Basic, somatosensory meditation
Fluid focus	Advanced, feeling meditation
Fluid focus	Advanced, autogenic analysis
Global focus	Advanced, inner-outer world

3.

WORDS, CONCEPTS, AND LIFE

The well-known anecdote that Inuits have many different words for snow fits well with the idea that languages are created to name the many different experiences of the people who speak them. If this is so, the lack of a single English word to express what is called *erlebnis* in German or *vivencia* in Spanish may suggest that Anglo-Saxons, such a practical people, have little use for the subtle nuances of spiritual life. Yet, those nuances exist and form the essence of our human experience. As we see later, words are the handles we use to collect and combine concepts, so, for lack of a more concise term, we shall call the spiritual nuances we will be talking about "live-experience."

To get to a definition of live-experience, let us begin with the more familiar concept of "experience." If we dive deep into its meaning, we realize that it refers at least to three different concepts: one is the number of skills or knowledge acquired through practice, such as in "I have medical experience" or "I have a lot of experience with children." The second is the straightforward and continuous perception of rather neutral relevance, like in "I experience cold in the hand when you put the ice on it." The third meaning is the subjective, embodied, immediate understanding of something. This type of experience, usually remembered as something that creates in us a strong and lasting impression, is a live-experience.[34]

Let us clarify the process with a practical exercise: if I close my eyes and say "mother" (a word), notions of motherhood and genealogy may come to mind (concepts), and I may get images of my own mother, coupled with warm feelings of tenderness and gratitude and some flashes of self-understanding (live-experience).

The words and the concepts are nearly the same for all of us, yet the live-experiences have a highly personal quality. Sharing live-experiences requires an effort, not always easy. Words can be said or written; concepts can be defined. Live-experiences can only be felt, or, better, lived.

If you like to, you may stop now before you continue your reading, and give it a try in the way I just did. Start with some word that appeals to you and follow all the way from the word to the concept to the live-experience. Unless you have a better idea, I propose you try "mother," and see what you get. If you intend to become a serious meditator, I suggest that you write down what happens and keep it for your records.

You may say at this point that a live-experience is like the feeling that comes with an important idea or a memory, and you are right. There is something more to it though, such as body sensations and even movements, visceral reactions, deep thoughts, and, most importantly, a sense of understanding, of immediacy, of being in touch with something real and meaningful. By the way, every feeling has a name (word), a definition (concept), and a live-experience.

Once, many years ago, I asked Wolfgang Luthe about a technical detail of the new psychotherapeutic method he was developing. He smiled and said, "I will explain this to you as soon as you understand it." I thought he was playing with words, so I took his answer as a joke and forgot about the question. Years later, as I was falling asleep on a plane after a long trip, the sudden revelation of what Luthe meant startled me awake: When I posed the question, I was expecting the oral transmission of concepts; yet, Luthe felt that the answer I needed was a change of attitude, not a piece of theory. Some things can be learned only through live-experience; the more you talk about them before you have a living understanding of them, the more confused you get. What I understood is that the essence of his method was not in the technical details, but in the underlying principle. If you understand the principle, you can describe and apply the method in many different ways.[35]

Reviewing the process, the first step to consider is from the word to the concept. Words by themselves are of little value. Some words may sound beautiful, but what is important is the concept to which the word leads, that is, the meaning of the word. Some speakers say lots of words, which may sound even right, but if you come to think of it, you are not sure what they are talking about. At times, even you may use a word without knowing what you precisely mean. It is a good practice, when you are reading, stop anytime you find a word you do not understand and look it up in a dictionary. I even have etymological dictionaries, which lead me from the current meaning of the word to its roots, origins, and changes through cultural history.

Of course, do not overdo it, but it is interesting to explore some words, particularly those with high human power. Take the word "love," for instance. Everybody knows what it means, or so they think, but in fact, there are many and even opposite meanings. A lot of confusion is created by the use of this word. In my system, love is a technical concept clearly defined and classified in its many varieties. Do not worry, at some point, I will help you to differentiate between love and attachment, between conditional and unconditional love, between nurturing love, admiring love, sharing or interactive love, and so on.

However, even if you have a clear concept of something, this may still be an empty concept. Concepts do not have life. You have life, you are life, and only you can give life to a concept. Go back to love and feel it. The life-experience of love is going to be part of your training, so it is all right to check now your baseline. I have no idea how love feels like to you. Do you feel sexually aroused?[36] Do you feel like caring for someone? Do you feel admiration or gratitude? Does it come as concern about what he or she may be doing? Do you feel despondent because love, precisely, is what you need and nobody loves you? Write down your live-experience of love at this moment and keep it in your records.

We may also do the process in reverse, going from the live-experience to the word. Some live-experiences are difficult to describe. At times, we cannot find the right words, or we may explain our live-experience in a way nobody seems to understand. This is a problem well known to mystics and to highly creative people. But with some training, you will develop the ability to find precise (more or less) words for clear (more or less) concepts that link well with your live-experiences. Training in this process will lead you to increased understanding of yourself and your circumstances.

The Mug Metaphor

We can summarize all this discussion by a practical metaphor: take a mug by its handle and get some coffee, tea, broth, or whatever inside. Sip a little bit and put it aside. Think about what you have just done and tell me: what is more important, the mug, its handle, or the broth?

Right, all are important. You need a container for the broth, and the handle comes handy to sip from it. Of course, both are meaningless without the broth. The handle is the word; the container is the concept to which the word is attached like the handle is attached to the mug, and the broth sipping is the live-experience. Any mug will do, even without a handle, if the broth is good. The most beautiful collection of china cups is just decoration if you have no broth (tea, coffee…) to put inside.

Some Training with Living Words

Say the word "bus." You know what a bus is; it is a clear concept in your mind. Now close your eyes and remember any time you were in a bus. Are you seating or are you standing, feeling your grip in the bus bar? It may come the last time or the first time, or anytime you were on a bus. It may be a dramatic time: Were you ever in a bus accident? Did you ever meet a special person on a bus? Or maybe you are just getting a dull, boring ride.

Now, do you get the idea? I am asking you to live what it is like to ride in a bus. Imagine that you have never been on a bus; then it is going to be difficult to get the live-experience. Even if I were the most experienced bus passenger in the world and I were to explain thousand times to you how it is like to ride on a bus, it will still be difficult for you to get into the life-experience. You may rehearse it in your mind; you may get some vicarious experience. You may believe that you know how been on a bus feels like. But only when you finally get into a real bus, something will light up inside you, you get an internal luminous click, and realize that what you are living in that particular moment is the live-experience of a bus. All your readings and lectures about buses come to you, and then you say, "Wow, so this is the bus experience Luis de Rivera was talking about."

I know the example of the bus is a bit silly, but never mind, I did it on purpose. There is nothing special about live-experiences; it is something very common and simple. I only mention it so much because I have seen people talking about things like "cosmic feeling," "illumination," "mindfulness," and "compassion," in a way that reveals vague concepts and self-indulgent imaginations. There is nothing bad about that. It is like a nice collection of empty china cups. It is all right to collect china cups, as it is all right getting into self-indulgent *revèries*, provided that in both cases you know what you are doing.

The coherent connection between word, concept, and live-experience is not always present in our normal life. It may not matter much if we miss those links on things like buses or carrots, but training in mindfulness requires making the right links all the time. It is an experiential process and having the right connections among words, concepts, and live-experiences is essential.

Learning words and concepts is of some, but not much, use. You need to connect them with a real live-experience. Some scholars know a lot of words and can give precise definitions of most of them but have no life-experience of what they are talking about. The purpose of this book is to guide you into the live-experience of meditation, not to teach you philosophy, religion, and the like. Nevertheless, we need some theoretical background, just to know what our words mean. So, I will next give you some definitions of words that you will be reading all along this book. You may already have the live-experience, and connecting with the corresponding concept will make you happier and more secure. Remember, the broth needs a cup. The concept is the cup. Your live-experience is the broth. Words are just handles.

More Useful Words

Just read the words and make sure that you understand the concept. If you sense the live-experience, that is, if the concept reveals something that you have lived, something that you have practical personal experience with, this is very fine. If not, just learn the concept and wait. The live-experience will come and, when it does, you will recognize it. Do not try to learn anything by heart. Just read it lightly and come back to it when you need to.

Anxiety: Fearful expectation. An unpleasant feeling that something bad is about to happen. When the "bad thing" is going on right now, anxiety is called anguish, or "panic."

Relaxation: The experience of security and absence of danger. A pleasant feeling that everything is all right and nothing bad can possibly happen.

Stress: A demand that exceeds the performance level at which you feel comfortable.

Mindfulness: Full concentration for *shamata* meditation, full awareness for *vipassana* meditation. Modern vulgar use, full attention to everything in general and nothing in particular. The seventh path of Buddha's Noble Eightfold Path and passive acceptance in autogenics.

Meditation: To measure something mentally. In old Christianity, concentrating your attention on God. English for the Sanskrit Dhyana, the Pali Jhana, the Chinese Ch'an, and the Japanese Zen. The eighth path of Buddha's Noble Eightfold Path and passive concentration in autogenics.

Transcendence: Live-experience that goes beyond the usual limits of ordinary experience. The feeling of intimate contact with an entity larger than oneself.

Autogenic: Generated by oneself. Structures and dynamics created and/or regulated by intrinsic processes.

Training: Skillful repetitions of a technique until its results become automatic.

Technique: A well-described procedure, which produces standard observable results.

Active concentration: Focus attention on something to get a specific result.

Passive concentration: Focalizing attention on a particular object, idea, image, sensation, and so on, without any demand, expectation, or controversy.

Passive acceptance: Receptive awareness of something as it is. Being aware without expectation, evaluation, judgment, or intent to change.

Dual concentration: The specific meditation method of autogenics. Consists on passive concentration in the same experience by two paths: (1) the direct perception of a somatic sensation and (2) the concurrent verbalization of the somatosensory experience that is taking place.

Mental contact: Awareness of a part of the body and of the sensations coming from it.

Sensation: The live-experience of a body activity.

Emotion: The immediate experience of rejection or approach. Corresponds to the first step of feeling.

Feeling: The dynamic development of emotion. An opinion made by the limbic system about the circumstances.

Attention Management Training: A standardized procedure registered by Luis de Rivera for developing attentional processes.

Daydreaming: To set up a movie on your mind. Visually imagining a story, usually pleasant.

Revèrie: French for daydreaming. Allowing thoughts and images to evolve without any guide. Word made of literary value by Rousseau, who claimed to conceive his writings in a mental state of *revèrie*.

Faith: Believing something because somebody you trust told you.

Science: Doubting something you know firsthand because you may miss some facts.

First Autogenic Switch: change from ergotropic dominance to trophotropic dominance during the autogenic state.

Second Autogenic Switch: change from left-brain hemispheric dominance to right-brain hemispheric dominance during the autogenic state.

Metaphor: An expression that helps you to understand something, generally through a concrete concept that leads to the same live-experience than a more abstract concept.

Mug metaphor: The handle is the word, the cup is the concept, and the live-experience is the broth.

Tree metaphor: The body is the roots, the feeling the trunk, the thoughts the leaves, and the actions the fruits.

Paraphora: A phrase or word that takes you to a live-experience not related by meaning but by live-experience association. Example: "my heart beats" = "I am anxious"; "unconscious mechanisms" = "you are Freudian.". Also an obsolete term to designate minor mental disorder.

4.

ATTENTION MANAGEMENT TRAINING

Without much effort, you are naturally aware of your surroundings, which are outside of you so we may say that they form your external world. You are also conscious of the creations of your own mind, such as your thoughts, memories, feelings, and sensations, which are inside you so we will call all those your inner world. Let us imagine that you could be aware of everything that happens both in your internal and in your external worlds at the same time (which you are not because that would require an enormous brain-processing capacity), but, if you were, you wouldn't need attention.

Natural Attention

Attention is the human ability to focus awareness on a given object or circumstance, more or less disregarding the rest. You were born with this ability, which is the same than saying that you are able to decide what you do want to be aware of.

Perhaps the word "decide" is not exact enough. Most of the time, you do not decide anything about your attention; it just gets drawn away from you into this or that object or happening. Who decides where does your attention go? Let us remember our previous discussion about the "radar" property of our ancestor's attention in chapter 2. Not paying attention to anything is very relaxing, as attention requires effort. But if a menacing sound happens, your attention gets immediately drawn to this part of the external world that may need some fixing. You have in your genetic line many ancestors with this spontaneous reaction (those who did not have it would hardly survive in a wild environment, so they were not likely to leave many offspring).

At another moment, a small rabbit, not dangerous at all, may have happened to pass running by one of your ancestors; his attention, particularly if he was hungry, got immediately drawn to it, and, if he managed to hunt and eat the rabbit, he would survive. If he was good at that, he was also likely to leave many offspring, one of them probably you. Therefore, it was Mother Nature, through her evolutionary laws, who decided that your attention is to be drawn both to dangerous and to appetizing things.

Now, let us say that you want to make your own personal decisions about what to pay or not to pay attention to. But, why would you want to do that? One simple reason is that you are forced to do it. Remember your first day at school. As a natural child, you were interested in, say, flies gliding over your head, the blond hair of the girl in the first row, and the bizarre noises the kid in the back row was making. As you were doing that, a stern voice called your name. Your attention shifted to a grown-up who was looking at you with a serious face. "What was I saying?" she asked. Of course, you did not know. "You are not paying attention; you were distracted," she said. That was the most important lesson you ever learned in school: you have to pay attention. Do not allow yourself to be distracted.

Soon you discovered that paying attention had many advantages, other than appeasing your teacher: it enabled you to learn many new and exciting things, you could decipher strange signs that became a source of information and entertainment, you could manipulate complex objects, and you could become skilled at many different arts. Do not hold any resentment to your stern teacher, she or he introduced you to a most exclusive human ability: attention management. Incidentally, I believe that the current epidemic of attention deficit disorder has its origins in the gradual extinction of stern teachers at the hands of permissive theories about the importance of allowing the unfolding of the natural child. Those theories are right, but they forget that the potentialities of the natural child have to be trained to be of any use. To put an extreme example, humans do have the natural ability to talk, but they would never be able to do so if nobody talks to them when they are little. To be more extreme, babies have the natural ability to live, but they will die if nobody nurses them.

Coming back to the pleasure of learning new things, you discover here another natural human tendency: curiosity, which is the craving for new information. Your brain does have more computing power that the one needed to process monotonous well-known surroundings, so it tends to expand its external world by exploring new environments and also to expand its inner world by creating new concepts and new combinations of old concepts. So, to summarize, we can say that natural attention is activated by danger, by pleasure, and by curiosity.

Managed Attention

The wish to control attention is activated first by the external pressure of education, and then by the discovery that the natural functions of your attention perform better if you make the effort of concentrating on the task at hand. Now you are in the position to decide if you want to be the master of your attention, which is the first step to being the master of your mind, or if you prefer to allow life to push you around, drawing your attention from a brilliant goody to the next. Take your time to be sure that you make the decision to be the master of your mind. As soon as you make this decision, you are ready to start your Attention Management Training. All it takes from here is to keep your choice alive and get a skilled external teacher. If you put the decision,[37] as you read this how-to-do-it book, I will provide the teaching.

Natural attention could be free, that is, fully available and not fixed into anything, or captured, that is, drawn and fixed to a given stimulus. If fixed, the fixation could be unshakable, with absolute disregard for any other incentive, or brittle and jumping from one thing to another to another. The first possibility, unshakably fixed attention, produces a mind state we call "trance" and the second possibility, jumpy attention, a mind state we call "distraction." There is a continuum of many states in the middle, each one of them located at some point between the two extremes of trance and total distraction. As soon as you have the intent of graduating your absorption level, or what is the same, your distraction level, you are managing your attention.

Keeping your attention stable at your desired point in the absorption-distraction continuum is concentration. If your attention waves too much, your concentration is no good, but do not worry, it is only a matter of training.

When you keep your attention stable for a while, you may begin to feel bored and sleepy. Therefore, your second task in managing attention is to keep yourself awake; your awareness has to be as vivid as if you had just discovered the object in which you are concentrating.

Never mind if the great psychologist William James said that it is impossible to maintain vivid attention in an object that does not change: this is only true for natural attention. The yogis who trained Buddha before he discovered *vipassana* were able to do it for days. You will learn to maintain your attention both stable and vivid, but do not expect to do it for more than a few minutes in a row. This mode of concentration is *samatha*, defined as "the faculty of sustaining the attention upon a familiar object without being distracted away from it."[38]

Do not think that you are failing if your attention wavers at times away from the focus. This happens, even to advanced meditators. In fact, there are more aspects in the concentration exercise than just concentrating. Meditation practice trains several aspects of attention:

(1) maintaining your attention focused on the experience;
(2) awareness of mental activity extraneous to the focus;
(3) restraining yourself to be lured away from the focus into extraneous activity (passive acceptance);
(4) catching yourself when distracted;
(5) abandoning the distraction; and
(6) returning to focalized attention.

The Right Concentration

Concentration requires an object, which can be of many different types. Anything can serve as a focus for concentration. The first distinction shall be between external focus, such as an object and a flame, and an internal focus, such as a sensation, a feeling, and a mental image.

The second distinction is whether the focus is global, as total awareness of the complete field of perception, or selected. The selected focus can be static, as an image or a sound, or fluid, as the trend of thoughts or the changing nuances of feelings. Finally, the focus can be variable, what means that there is no stable focus and that you are daydreaming.

Some meditators claim to concentrate on "silence," or on "the void," or "in the space between thoughts"—that is, to produce a concentration without an object. Rather than this being a method, I think they are referring to the final experience of all methods, which possibly corresponds to the nirvana experience.

Different schools of meditation specialize in a different focus, but I will not get into details now. For a comparative study of meditation methods, please check for my forthcoming book *The Many Ways of Mindfulness*, available soon on Amazon.

More essential for meditation are the different ways of concentrating. Whereas any focus may do, there is only one right concentration for meditation.

CONCENTRATION FOCUS BY MEDITATION SCHOOL

FOCUS	SCHOOL
Global	Zen
Static	Samatha
Fluid	Vipassana
Variable	Daydreaming

The first kind of concentration, the one you learned at school, the one you use now to succeed in your everyday tasks, is no good for meditation. It will not lead you to mindfulness and to the relaxation response. If anything, it will stress you more. Luthe called it *active concentration* because it is excellent for action and achievement. The purpose of active concentration is achieving or avoiding something, that is, it is bent in obtaining results, not any result, but a particular result that is more or less known beforehand. Active attention is always accompanied, therefore, by scanning and by evaluation of the results obtained by the effort. If you are doing, say, mental calculus and you concentrate in the sum of 354 plus 872, you want to make sure that the ciphers add up to 1226. If the results are correct, your teacher will nod happy at you, and you will feel good. If not, you will feel dejected and frustrated.

The right concentration is what Luthe called *passive concentration*; in opposition to the active kind, in passive concentration, there is no intent, wish, or purpose to achieve or to avoid anything in particular. Why would you make the effort of fixating your attention if there is nothing to gain or lose and if everything matters the same? You may as well allow your mind to wander at its fancy, as many people do when they say that they are relaxing. This is passive, right, but is not concentration. Scattered concentration is not meditation.

TYPES OF CONCENTRATION

BY MODE	BY FOCUS
Active	Static
Passive Receptive	Dynamic
Passive Scattered	Global
Dual	Diffuse

You may have had a glimpse at passive concentration watching the sea or the forest, or perhaps a campfire or even a work of art. I fancy that prehistoric men discovered passive concentration while gazing at a campfire and that the first meditation techniques evolved from there. In fact, one of the oldest yoga practices involves concentration in the flame of a lamp or candle. Passive concentration is a concept difficult to grasp and even harder to incorporate as a live-experience; that's why I explain passive concentration so many times in this book. But don't worry, it's like skating on ice. In the beginning, just to stand put seems impossible, then, after a while, you would slip awkwardly, and if you keep practicing, you might end up gliding like an Olympian star.

Passive Acceptance

Passive acceptance is a most necessary complement to passive concentration. Once you learn it, you see it as an obvious corollary, but the likes are that you would not think of it if I do not tell you. Even seasoned meditators may fail to apply it in their practice, which does much improve when they do. Before we get into the topic, tell me: What would you do if strange thoughts or images come to your mind whereas you are applying the right concentration in your chosen focus?

If you reject the strange ideas, you are paying attention to them; it may be negative attention, but it is attention nevertheless. If you accept them and allow your attention to be taken by them, you lose your focus, and your meditation is spoiled. This is what Luthe told me after I failed to find the correct answer to the question:

Accept the strange elements as if you were interested in them, while, at the same time, you have no interest whatsoever in them.

If it sounds to you like cryptic Taoist yin-yang jargon, this may be because you do not have the passive acceptance live-experience yet. Keep working on the concept, bring it with you in your practice, and soon it will become evident. Acceptance means that everything is all right, that whatever happens is what precisely was meant to happen. In active concentration, you only accept what fits your expectations; in passive concentration, you accept anything and everything that comes to mind and, at the same time, do not care about the nature of what you are accepting. You avoid any evaluation, critique, judgment, in sum, any interaction with the alien contents of your mind. In colloquial terms, you pass, that is why it is called passive acceptance.

What about if what comes up is that your house is burning down? In all technical purity, you pass off or ignore the mental images of the fire, of your fear or of whatever comes to your mind, that is, of all mental contents strange to your chosen focus, but, of course, you do not pass of external circumstances of vital importance. By all means, get up and extinguish the fire. One of the beneficial effects of meditation is that you develop the sense of discrimination between those circumstances that need change and those that do not really matter. But this applies only to the external world; while you are meditating, everything is all right and nothing matters *in your internal world.*

5.

TRAINING YOUR BRAIN

Every single mind function you need in autogenics, your brain has been doing it all the time by itself; otherwise, you would not be alive now. Your brain maintains the constancy of the inner balance of your body (homeostasis), secures its adaptation to the ever-changing external situations (allostasis), regulates the growth, the development, and the repair of your tissues, and ensures your well-being and your place in society.

Training in autogenics would enable you to activate essential brain regions on purpose and increase the efficiency of your brain. You must put some effort into it, as you would do in any training program. The therapeutic effect of autogenics is due to the enhancement of neuronal communication and of integration at all levels of brain function. Classic physiological studies in autogenic training show that the functional changes induced by the autogenic exercises become stable and permanent after six months of training (more or less). So, it's important that you promise to yourself being very consistent in following the program at least during the first six months of training. Do not worry for afterward, by that time autogenics would be such a part of you that you would enter the autogenic state just by thinking about it.

Our recent studies by brain functional magnetic resonance imagining (fMRI, for short) show which brain areas are activated during basic autogenic concentration,[39] confirming the hypothesis Schultz and Luthe had made many years before fMRI was invented. Studies with other meditation methods show similar changes in brain activation so that we can now say that attention training is also a way of training the brain. This makes sense, as you need your brain to use your attention, but, what is more important, the autogenic way to use your attention activates and develops brain areas related to emotion management and general health maintenance.

How You Got Your Brain(s)

We do not know how life came to be, but we know that once started, it kept evolving from the simplest forms to the immensely complicated ones. From the snail *Aplysia*[40] to the *Homo sapiens*, living beings have been solving their survival problems, interacting with the environment, and forming alliances/misalliances among themselves in increasingly complex ways. This has been possible, among other things, by the evolution of the brain, the main information-processing living structure, which evolved from groupings of a few isolated neurons to the billions of active interactive cells that form the human brain.

The first try for a brain was very efficient to keep homeostasis, that is, the inner constancy of body processes in the face of ever-changing external circumstances. Today, there remain some animals still functioning with this brain, like the snakes, the alligators, the crocodiles (this is why it is known as the "reptilian brain"). Those animals know very well how to feed themselves and how to maintain their body alive for as long as possible.

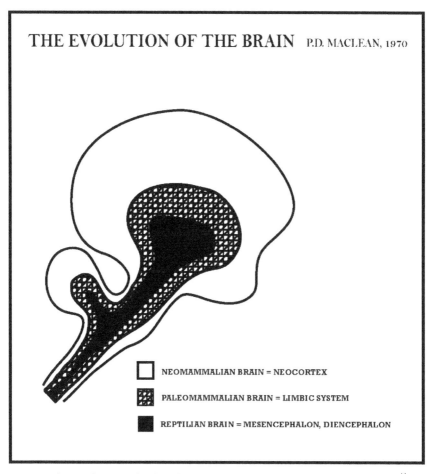

Figure from Luis de Rivera, *Psiconeuroendocrinologia*, 1981[41]

The reptiles are not very good at forming relationships or at learning new things. If they remain together is because they did happen to be born at the same place, but they never achieve any degree of social organization. They even eat each other if the opportunity arises and seem unable to cooperate. Mother Nature kept this brain because it was excellent at what it was doing, but in the course of time created a second brain, which evolved around the reptilian brain.

The second brain was good at recognizing people and at differentiating the friendly from the unfriendly, the dangerous from the inoffensive, those who have to be helped from those who better disappear. It was also very good at learning, especially those things that were necessary for survival and procreation. This brain grew around the first brain in the early mammals; now it is in full operation in rats, dogs, and many such animals, you name them. The mammal brain is good at forming relationships and so is very active in all social species. This second brain, physically located around the first reptilian brain, evaluates every circumstance regarding its significance to the continuity of a safe and happy life. If the circumstance seems no good, the evaluation is negative, and if it feels beneficial, the evaluation is positive. So, animals with this brain feel attracted to favorable circumstances and reject unbeneficial ones. Just watch your pet, and you see the mammalian brain in action.

The third brain is formed around the simple mammal brain and is capable of incredible feats; however, I wonder why Mother Nature allowed it to appear. To start with, the neo-mammalian brain, which is sizable only in anthropoids and, most and foremost, in humans, can process realities that do not exist and can create things that nature never thought of, such as cars, skyscrapers, mortgages and romantic love.

The computing ability of this new brain is so enormous that it gets bored processing average external reality and has to create complex inner worlds made of dreams, fantasies, and projects. Driven by their brainpower, humans have changed the earth in a few thousand years more than nature in millions, and most of this change has been made in the last century. Humans are even able to interfere with their own evolution. The rules and artifacts we create sharply separate us from the more normal animals.

It is good to remember that we still have, under our hyper sophisticated cortex, a reptilian brain that governs our bodily existence and a mammalian brain that regulates our affections, our feelings, our emotions. In reality, the whole picture is a bit more complicated, but for practical purposes, we can consider our brain divided into three sub-brains, richly interconnected but relatively able to function independently.[42]

Each human sub-brain is a revised version of a previous step in brain evolution, kept in place because it fulfilled very well its functions, while evolution was adding new sub-brains for additional tasks.

Traditional education and psychotherapy rely very much on the cognitive processes of the third brain while disregarding and even despising the other two. But you should not overindulge in the enthusiasm for the cognitive functions.

The truth is that you need a lot of training for your hypothalamus and for your limbic system, which is not provided by our culture. Do not worry, Autogenics will teach you how to do it.

The division proposed by MacLean is not as neat as it seems, and some scholars have contested it, although without contributing anything better. It is true that all the brain structures are so densely interconnected that several cooperative networks could be described, such as the ergotropic-trophotropic division of Hess,[43] but none has the powerful explanatory value of MacLean's triune brain hypothesis.[44]

The three brain structures of MacLean are meant to cooperate, to the point of performing together as a unified entity. However, at times they may work at great odds with each other. The disharmony among the three brains is more frequent in persons with psychosomatic or neurotic disorders; in fact, many scientists say this in reverse order, considering that such disorders are produced by discoordination among the different brain levels.

From the reptilian brain, you got the diencephalon, with its center in the hypothalamus, which is in charge of regulating the bare survival of your body. From the early mammalian brain, you got your limbic system or inner brain, starring the amygdala and the hippocampus, which is in charge of controlling your emotional life. From the greatly evolved neo-mammalian brain you got the neocortex, with its two brain hemispheres, which is in charge of controlling consciousness, perception, voluntary movements, cognitive processes, and intuition.

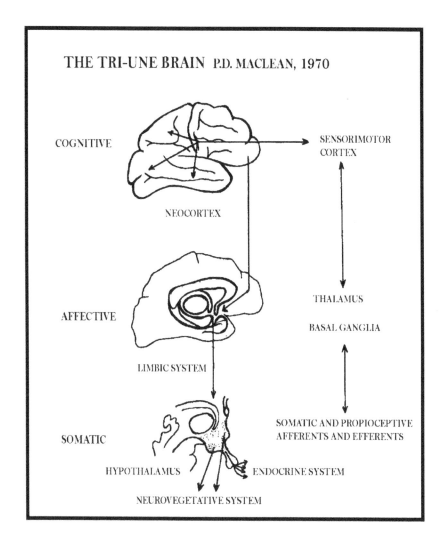

Figure from Luis de Rivera, *Psicosomatica*, 1980[45]

The information coming from the external world arrives at the cortex, the limbic system, and the diencephalon. The cortex performs rational operations, action planning, and anticipation of consequences. The limbic system registers the emotional meaning of information for survival and affiliation. The diencephalon regulates the instincts and coordinates neurovegetative and endocrine responses.

The Diencephalon

The Swiss doctor Walter Hess, not to be mistaken for the Nazi leader Rudolf Hess, won the Nobel Prize in 1949 for discovering that the diencephalon, the improved version of the reptilian brain, carries the central control of the integrated functions of all internal organs. Parts of the diencephalon are the reticular formation, which extends to the brain stem and regulates the level of consciousness, the thalamus that ensures the awareness of the information coming from the senses (except olfaction) and the hypothalamus that governs autonomic body functions. Hess's major contribution was the discovery of two behavioral systems in the hypothalamus, named ergotropic and trophotropic.

The ergotropic-trophotropic theory of Hess influenced researchers very relevant to meditation, such as Luthe, Gellhorn, and Roland Fisher.[46] All of them coincided that autogenics improve the "neurovegetative sintony," whose most important part is the working balance between the sympathetic and parasympathetic autonomic systems.

The ergotropic system (*Ergos* = work in old Greek) starts in the back of the hypothalamus and runs upward to the limbic system and the cortex, and downward to the sympathetic branch of the autonomic nervous system. It is in charge of functions that require effort and expense of energy, such as running or fighting, and thus accelerates your heart, raises your blood pressure, makes your muscles contract, and the like. The "stress reaction" described by Hans Selye[47] and the "fight or flight reaction," described by Walter Cannon,[48] are ergotropic responses.

The increase in ergotropic activity is very useful when you have to face a physical effort, not so much when the challenge is of psychological nature.

The trophotropic system (*trophos* = nutrition) starts in the front of the hypothalamus and runs upward to the limbic system and the cortex, and downward to the body through the parasympathetic branch of the autonomic nervous system. It is in charge of functions related to feeding and nourishing, resting, recovering of energy, and elimination of waste.

The trophotropic system takes care of all processes that recuperate energy, such as feeding, digesting, relaxing, and sleeping. It is also related to evacuation of waste, regulating functions such as voiding, urinating, and vomiting. This system is activated in humans by tender physical contact (as any loving mother knows) and by passive concentration (the reason why meditation is relaxing and recuperating).

The trophotropic system spreads through the body by the parasympathetic nervous system, entering in complementary balance with the sympathetic nervous system. Trophotropic activation reduces heart frequency, blood pressure, skin conductance, muscular tension, and the secretion of stress hormones. True to its nutritive function, it also increases the secretion of insulin, growth hormone, and oxytocin. Herbert Benson[49] called this integrated response, in all contrary to Selye's stress response, the "relaxation response," although we could well call it the "trophotropic response," or, as Heinrich Wallnöfer suggests, the "inverse arousal reaction."[50]

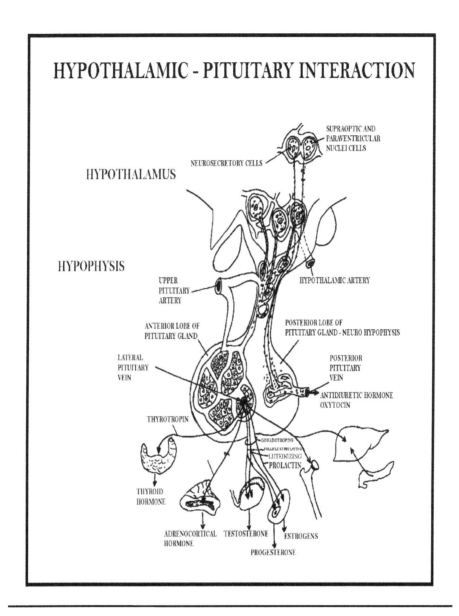

Figure from Luis de Rivera, *Psicosomatica*, 1980

The hypothalamic neuroendocrine cells control the adenohypophysis (anterior pituitary lobe) through a porta venous system and discharge its secretion directly in the neurohypophysis (posterior pituitary lobe).

The hypothalamus also coordinates the endocrine system, through its connection with the hypophysis, also known as the pituitary gland. The ergotropic system activates the secretion of hormones like ACTH, cortisol, thyroxin, adrenalin, and noradrenalin, the so-called stress hormones. The trophotropic system activates the secretion of the glucose-metabolizing hormone insulin, the "attachment hormone" oxytocin,[51] the growth hormone, and the gonadotrophins.[52]

In summary, the diencephalon oversees the "vegetative life," that is, the automatic functioning of the body and its "homeostasis" or adaptation to changing circumstances,[53] maintaining the constancy of temperature and the composition of body fluids. The hypothalamus also activates the external behaviors needed to maintain internal body functions, such as the fight-or-flight reaction,[54] sleep, hunger, thirst, and physical sex (just bare sex, nothing to do with affection or erotic desire).

It was an early discovery of autogenics that active concentration activates the ergotropic system, whereas passive concentration activates the trophotropic system.

Our normal life offers plenty of opportunities to train the ergotropic system because active concentration is our usual way of concentrating. In fact, we usually let our attention wander unless we want to achieve or avoid something or to produce some effect on the environment. Then, we apply active concentration to secure our aims.

In contrast, the opportunities to train the trophotropic system are few. This is why most of your normal life is carried out in a mild state of needless ergotropic activation, and this is also why the regular practice of autogenics is so important. Passive concentration trains the trophotropic system and increases basal trophotropic tonus. The increased trophotropic activity enters into flexible dynamic interplay with the already well-developed ergotropic activity, a phenomenon called "neuro-vegetative syntony." The normal waking state of the average person is of light to medium ergotropic activation, regardless of circumstances. The regular waking state of a person trained in autogenics adapts flexibly to circumstances, oscillating between light trophotropic and light ergotropic activation, according to the type of response required. This is why we say that regular practice of autogenics improves the neuro-vegetative sintony.

The autogenic exercises induce a particular state of mind, called the "autogenic state," which is interrupted at the end of the exercise by the standard termination procedure. When the autogenic state begins, there is a change from the usual active everyday mild ergotropic dominance to a stable mild trophotropic dominance. This shift, named "the autogenic switch" by Schultz, is now called the First Autogenic Switch (FAS), to differentiate it from the Second Autogenic Switch (SAS), the change from left-hemisphere dominance to right-hemisphere dominance which was described by Luthe. In long-trained individuals, FAS is almost immediate and can be produced even in the ordinary state by the simple recall of the autogenic state[55].

In untrained individuals, ergotropic activation is associated with alertness and trophotropic activation with sleep and slumber. Hess demonstrated the same effect in his experiments with cats, as they tended to fall asleep when the trophotropic region was stimulated. I call this the "sleep reflex of trophotropic activation" or "sleep trophotropic reflex," for short. The association between trophotropic activation and sleep is the resultant of the automatic cooperation between the hypothalamus and the reticular formation, a brain structure that runs from the upper-spinal medulla through the midbrain to end in the diencephalon.[56]

The reticular formation controls the levels of arousal and consciousness, which are, by default, associated to the trophotropic-ergotropic continuum—low arousal in the trophotropic end, high arousal in the ergotropic end. Training in autogenics involves inhibition of the sleep trophotropic reflex, which means that you train yourself to deactivate the connection between the trophotropic system and the reticular formation.

At variance of what happens in untrained individuals, after some training in autogenics, you will be able to dissociate the trophotropic state from the reticular formation reflex, if you want to. You can still fall asleep doing the exercise if this is convenient for you, at night in your bed, for instance. But at other times, you can stimulate the trophotropic system by passive concentration and maintain alertness, even in the middle of important trophotropic activation. The autogenic state and sleep are two different states, and falling asleep or allowing yourself to slack into slumber during the autogenic exercise is a technical error. Nevertheless, as it is easier to go into normal sleep from the autogenic state than from the waking state, you may release the "sleep trophotropic reflex" anytime you wish to fall fast into a peaceful sleep.

The Limbic System

Surrounding the diencephalon and inside the cortical brain is the limbic system, so called because it is the limit or margin between those two structures (i.e., the meaning of limbus in Latin: margin in between). Initially described by Papez, it was further studied by MacLean, who also advanced the idea that it is an improved version of the primitive mammalian brain.

The anatomical boundaries of the limbic system are relatively clear, but the richness of its connections to nearby parts of the brain keeps neuroscientists still discussing its functional boundaries. The limbic system is also called "the inner brain," because it is formed by the internal parts of both hemispheres, facing each other and surrounding the corpus callosum, the thick bundle of fibers that connects the two brain hemispheres.

Although there is still some discussion about which neuronal structures conform the limbic system, the evidence that its primary function is the regulation of emotions and feelings is overwhelming. A detailed description of the limbic system is beyond the scope of this book, but you should know a few facts about the vital structures trained by autogenics.

Richly connected with the diencephalon is the amygdala, a collection of small groupings of neurons involved in emotional reactions, at least of fear and anger.[57]

THE LIMBIC SYSTEM IN MEDIAL VIEW OF THE BRAIN

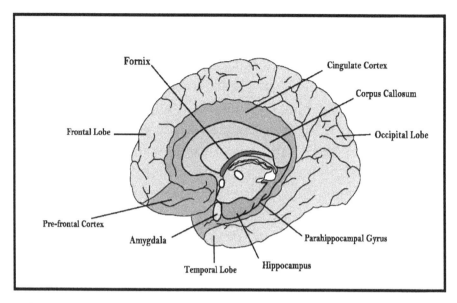

Figure modified from Kandel *Principles of Neural Science*, 1991

The cingulate cortex is a brain lobe in the internal part of each hemisphere, embracing in all its extension the corpus callosum. A bundle of fibers traverses the cingulate cortex conducting impulses from the amygdala to the cingulate neurons and ending in the prefrontal cortex, which is so richly connected to the cingulate cortex that some neuroscientists consider it now a part of the limbic system, at least functionally. The hippocampus is in the inner part of the temporal lobe and forms part of the limbic system, where it has as its main function the emotional activation of memories.

Whereas the fight-or-flight reactions are automatic body responses launched by the diencephalon, emotions are a more elaborated experience, initiated by the amygdala and transformed into feelings by the cingulate and the prefrontal cortex. Emotions are intermediate psycho-physiological experiences depending on the awareness of the activation of the diencephalic-limbic connection.[58]

The processing of emotions begins in the amygdala, continues through the cingulate cortex, and ends in the prefrontal cortex. Many collateral ancillary connections spill the limbic system activity over the rest of the brain, originating the many correlates of emotion. The better the limbic system performs the emotion-feeling process, the less disturbing emotional correlates appear. By the time the process is finished, the emotions have lost their quality of physical action-inducing experiences, evolving into the dynamic psychological experience we call "feeling." Feelings are opinions made by the limbic system, a concept basic to feeling meditation, to be tackled in chapter 8.

From clinical observation, it has been known for a long time that autogenic training improves emotional balance. We have been able to show very recently that the actual practice of the autogenic exercises activates the limbic system. This evidence was gathered by the Tenerife Autogenic Brain Scan Study—TABS—in which functional magnetic resonance imagining (fMRI) was performed in fifteen long-trained subjects during the autogenic state.[59] On conclusion, we are able to formulate the following hypothesis:

The repeated activation of key limbic structures by standard autogenic training is the neurobiological basis for the increased ability to appropriately handle feelings observed in individuals long trained in autogenics.

THE LIMBIC SYSTEM ACTIVATED BY AUTOGENICS

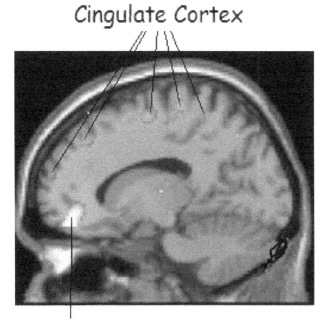

Cingulate Cortex

Pretrontal Cortex

Image from Luis de Rivera et al, 2017

fMRI view of the limbic system, showing activation of the cingulate cortex and the prefrontal cortex during the autogenic state. (TABS Study, 2017)

For color views of the TABS study, see

www.icat.world

The Brain Cortex

The cortex forms the outer part of the brain, surrounding the limbic system. The cortex centralizes conscious sensory information, integrates it with that stored in the memory and with the models of possible futures elaborated by the frontal lobes, and decides purposeful action. The central nervous system originates in the cortex (remember, the autonomic nervous system originates in the diencephalon). The neuronal fibers of the central nervous system take information from the sense organs and deliver instructions for action to all voluntary muscles.

The brain seen from above is an oblong organ divided by the *longitudinal fissure* in two halves, known as *brain hemispheres*. They are very similar in gross anatomical appearance but quite different in their ways of processing information. Another curious peculiarity is that each hemisphere receives and sends information to the opposite side of the body.

Decussation is the technical name for the crossing over of brain nerves from each hemisphere to the opposite side of the body. The *lemniscus decussation* is the crossing of the body sensory nerves, which takes place in the upper part of the medulla, and the *pyramidal decussation* is the crossing of the motor nerves, which takes place a little bit below. All the senses, but olfaction, are decussated[60]. The visual decussation, named optic chiasma, is a little weird, as the external retinal part of each eye connects with the same hemisphere and the medial part with the contralateral.

BRAIN HEMISPHERES UNITED BY THE CORPUS CALLOSUM

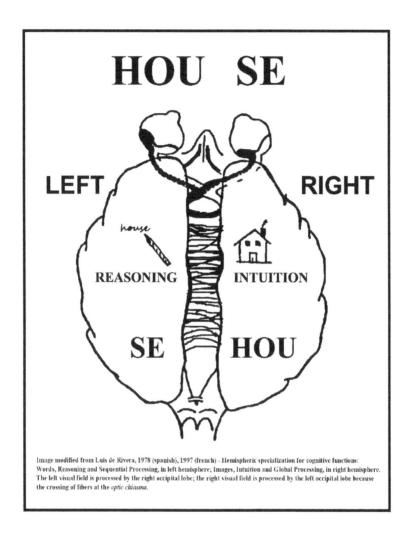

Image modified from Luis de Rivera, 1978 (spanish), 1997 (french) - Hemispheric specialization for cognitive functions: Words, Reasoning and Sequential Processing, in left hemisphere; Images, Intuition and Global Processing, in right hemisphere. The left visual field is processed by the right occipital lobe; the right visual field is processed by the left occipital lobe because the crossing of fibers at the *optic chiasma*.

The corpus callosum is the thick bundle of fibers connecting the two hemispheres, integrating the bilateral information and the two different modes of information processing: sequential (reasoning) and global (intuition)

Hemispheric Dominance

Most people, about 90 percent of the population according to classical estimates, are right handed. This means that their left-brain hemisphere controls most of their fine and useful movements, such as writing, picking things up, eating, and much more, while in about 10 percent of the population those functions are controlled by the right hemisphere. The hemisphere that controls the preferred hand is usually referred as the "dominant hemisphere." However, dominance also relates to leg control (you play soccer with your right or with your left foot?), eye preferences (you aim your rifle with the right or the left eye?), ear preferences (you answer the phone with your right or with your left ear?). The higher a hemisphere scores in dominance, the more likely is that it will also be in charge of speech and mathematical functions. Some people, especially left-handed people, have mixed dominance.

Cognitive Specialization of the Hemispheres.

The dominant hemisphere, in most people the left hemisphere, processes cognitive information in sequential, logical patterns and is good at finding cause-effect relationships and analyzing details. The non-dominant hemisphere, usually the right, is more apt for global perception, intuitive grasping of complex situations, body awareness, and creativity.

The brain areas responsible for speech are in the left hemisphere, which easily represents concepts by words and ciphers. The right hemisphere is unable to form words, so it has to represent everything as images or body sensations.[61]

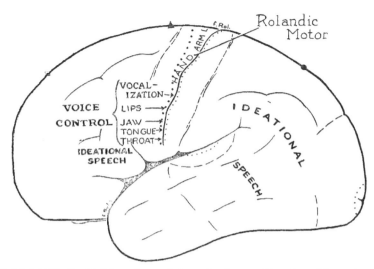

Penfield 1959. Left (dominant) hemisphere. Putting ideas into words (ideational speech) is done in Broca and Wernicke areas.

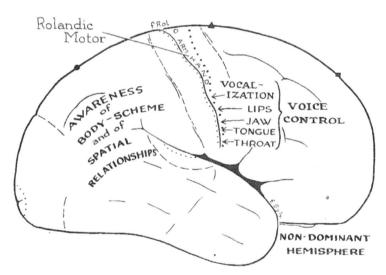

Penfield 1959. Right (nondominant) hemisphere. Processing of body awareness and spatial relationships.[62]

Second Autogenic Switch (SAS)

Schultz described an autogenic switch from ergotropic to trophotropic dominance during the autogenic state. Luthe proposed the occurrence of a second switch at the cortical level from left to right hemispheric dominance to explain the development of creativity in long-term autogenic trainees. Now, our fMRI studies confirm that there is a shift from the usual left-brain cognitive dominance to right-brain cognitive dominance during the autogenic state. The frequent repetition of the SAS enhances interhemispheric cooperation and explains other interesting effects of autogenics, like autogenic neutralization, increased self-awareness, the emergence of repressed memories, and the unification of consciousness.

RIGHT BRAIN ACTIVATION BY AUTOGENICS

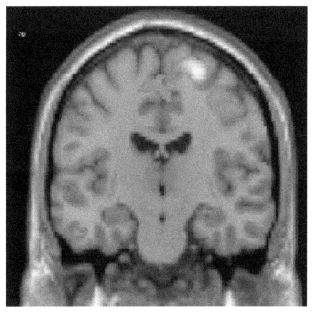

Activation of right frontal lobe and insula.
Luis de Rivera et al., TABS, 2017. **www.icat.world**

Motor and Somatosensory areas.

Body movements are controlled by the primary motor cortex, which runs vertically all through the frontal cortex, ahead of Rolando's fissure or central sulcus. Next behind, in the parietal cortex, runs the somatosensory area, which receives tactile and proprioceptive signals from the body. Because of the decussations, each hemisphere controls the movements and receives information from the opposite half of the body.

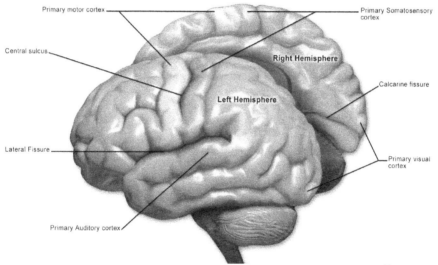

Motor and somatosensory primary cortexes (Blausen, 2014)[63]

The Penfield Homunculus.

The neurosurgeon Wilder Penfield mapped the distribution of the projections of the different parts of the body in the somatosensory cortex and in the motor cortex of the patients he was operating. The size of the brain projections does not correspond to actual body size but to the density of innervation of those body parts. The control and sensitivity of the face, for instance, occupies as much brain space as that of the whole trunk, and that of the fingers as much as that of the whole arm.[64]

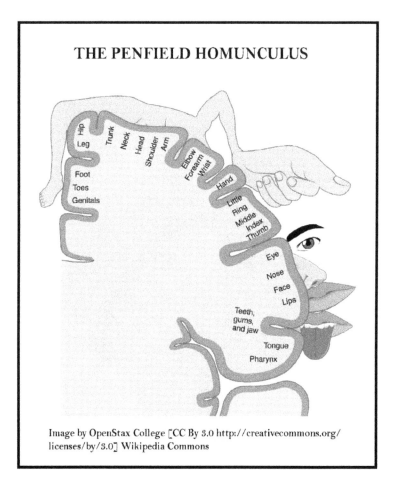

THE PENFIELD HOMUNCULUS

Image by OpenStax College [CC By 3.0 http://creativecommons.org/licenses/by/3.0] Wikipedia Commons

Training in basic autogenics increases all levels of brain connectivity and improves the neurovegetative sintony in the diencephalon, the emotional processing in the limbic system, and interhemispheric communication in the brain cortex

6.

GETTING INTO PRACTICE

This chapter gives you the basic instructions to prepare for the practice of autogenics, information also useful for practitioners of any other kind of meditation, as all of them train the same human faculties.

Reduce External Stimulation

In any mental activity, such as studying for your exams, preparing your next presentation at school or at the office, and so on, you would like a quiet atmosphere around you. The same is true with autogenics, except for a little detail that I will explain soon. Meanwhile, as you would with any other activity that requires concentration, make things easy for you. Avoid noisy places, try to be alone in a closed room where nobody would enter, reduce bright lighting, turn off phones, computers, and the like…but do not overdo it. It is much more important to develop *Passive Incidental Acceptance*

Passive Incidental Acceptance

It is all right to take appropriate care of securing your time and place for practice, but do not get too hooked to the formalities of reducing external stimulation. Do not get hysterical if somebody shouts outside your window, or if the TV in the living room is too loud. Do not leave your chair and go to silence your children. If you forgot to turn off your cellular and it rings insistently, do not chide yourself, nor jump to answer it or to silence it. Let it be, and keep training. This is incidental passive acceptance; the little detail I did mention before. *Incidental passive acceptance* differentiates training in autogenics to any other kind of mental training and is one of the little details that make autogenics so unique. I call it incidental because the opportunity is not planned; its occurrence is unexpected, *incidental*. You make use of this incident as an opportunity to progress in your training by practicing passive incidental acceptance.

You transform every disruption, big or small, into an opportunity to progress in your training.

You know what passive acceptance is—look up the definition up if you wish—disruptions are your opportunity to live-experience passive acceptance in difficult conditions. Pleasant, calm, soothing circumstances are easy to accept; disturbing, noisy, unpleasant incidents are not easy to accept, yet passive acceptance is always the same. The technique does not depend on how much you like what is going on in your experience.

You could also use the incident to get mad, to lose concentration, to berate yourself, or to start thinking about anything that fancies you. That is all right; there are many choices. I just want you to know that one of the choices is to benefit from the incident to improve your training on passive acceptance.

But, what about if you forgot that you have the option and you find yourself getting distracted or disturbed by some interruption? Well, as soon as you realize that you are distracted or indulging in your disturbance, remember you have the choice and go back to the passive-acceptance attitude. I will tell you more about how to handle distractions toward the end of this chapter.

Music and Guided Meditation

Some people say that they concentrate better with some little music, and that is fine, I have tried it and I like it. There is a whole chapter in my book *The Many Ways of Mindfulness* on how to use music to obscure other external stimuli and to deactivate inner distracting thoughts. You can relax very comfortably listening to your favorite music anytime you want to, but this is not autogenics.

Autogenics is to self-induce a state that increases your perception of all the phenomena generated by yourself. Research has also shown that this state improves the self-regulatory processes of the organism, which provides an extra meaning to the word. The whole idea of autogenics is to get in touch with yourself, that is, with everything that originates inside of yourself. Music comes from outside yourself so do not play music in autogenic meditation.

Planned or incidental concentration on external stimulation may be a worthwhile meditation method but is not autogenics. Turn your music player off, but if some distracting music happens to sound while you are in your meditation, just apply to it the incidental passive-acceptance technique.

For the same reasons, we will not use records to guide our autogenic meditation. This would spoil the "autogenic," that is, self-generated, part. I know that guided meditations are much in use, that they induce fascinating states, and that they may provide fantastic insights and transformations. Nevertheless, again, the whole idea of autogenics is to train your own capacity to produce a particular state of consciousness, the autogenic state. Some autogenic teachers may, to help you to learn the exercises, do them aloud with you at the beginning, or they may say something while you are concentrating, just to assist you in the learning process, but that is all. Once you know how to do the autogenic exercises, you keep training fully on your own.

Body Posture

Once you have secured the adequate environment, you go to the first practical training step: body position. The three basic postures in autogenics are regular sitting, lying down, and the coachman position. During the concentration in autogenous body sensations, it is best to minimize non-autogenous body stimulation, such as that produced by tight garments, shoes, belts, and other body attachments, like watches, heavy jewelry, and eyeglasses. As training progresses, any discomfort or extraneous sensations may be used to practice the passive-acceptance attitude, but in the beginning make things easy for yourself.

The regular sitting posture is the usual Western way of sitting in a comfortable chair or armchair. Fill the seat with your buttocks, rest your back on the backrest, support your arms on the arms of the chair or, if the chair does not have arms or this posture does not feel comfortable, rest your hands and wrists on your lap. If the back of the chair is long enough, you may rest your neck on it, but it is usually preferable to allow the head to tilt forward slightly.

The well-known yoga lotus posture, so much recommended for serious meditation today, originated in ancient India, where it is still in use among the peasant population. It is not seen so much in the cities now, but, if you go to some small villages, you will still find people sitting cross-legged in their living room, chatting in the most amiable way. They learn this posture in early childhood and practice it all the time; it is for them the usual way of seating. The same can be said about the Zen sitting position, *Seiza* (literally, proper sitting) still practiced by traditional people in Japan.

If you have long experience with the yogi and the *seiza* postures, feel very comfortable with them and do not have a good chair handy, you may do the training sitting this way. One of the practical advantages of the oriental sitting position is that it is very difficult to fall asleep on it while you are meditating. The main disadvantage for Westernized people is that it forces joints into a painful and at times damaging effort. After a lot of training, you may be able to keep passive acceptance hanging from a tree, but, in the beginning, make things easy for yourself.

The lying position is also very simple. Stretch yourself on your back on the floor or upon a blanket or mat. Keep the body symmetrical, arms alongside the body, legs straight. Your ordinary bed may do, only make sure that you do not fall asleep. The effects of the exercise are more powerful on the lying position than in the other positions.

This means that you reach more quickly a deep autogenic state, but also that you perceive better your distracting thoughts and memories and that you are more likely to get autogenic discharges. So, before trying the lying position, it is best to get some practice in the normal sitting position. Wait until you are sure that you dominate the method well enough not to get lost in your distractions or to fall asleep before you try the lying position.

The coachman position receives its name after the posture of an idle driver on his coach seat. Having nothing to do but wait, and lacking backrest, the coachman would allow his body to bend to ease tension on his spine and may even fall asleep in this position. The lower part of the body is firmly secured by the triangle formed by the seat and the two feet. The top of the body maintains itself stable by keeping its center of gravity in the center of the arc formed by the spine, bent neither too forward nor too backward, to keep in balance without muscle tension. This posture comes handy when you happen to do your training in unusual places, such as a bathroom or why not, in a coachman seat. It is also worth trying it when there are too many distractions in the seating position.

Slumber, Sleep, and Body Relaxation

The continuous effort required to maintain the yogi or the *seiza* postures help the meditator to keep himself awake. In autogenic meditation, the body is allowed to follow its autogenous needs of the moment. As the autogenic state progresses, the muscles will usually get into deep relaxation, and the continuous brain stimulation produced by muscle tension will slowly fade away.

For many people, the release of brain regions stimulated by muscle tension is associated with sleep, and they may experience this muscle relaxation as a sense of slumber.

Practice is required to maintain passive acceptance of slumber and sleepiness while keeping passive concentration focused on the proprioceptive live-experience. Falling asleep is a distraction, as it is a distraction getting involved in any mental activity other than the passive concentration in the proprioceptive or interoceptive sensations.

Keeping the slumber distraction away is easier in the sitting position, so that is why I recommend practicing a lot on this position before trying the lying position. The automatic muscle-relaxing effects of the autogenic state do also take place in the sitting posture, but they are not so strongly associated with slumber.

Both in the sitting and in the coachman positions, the body posture should be stabilized in such a way that no muscle tension is at all necessary to maintain it. Certain parts of the body might slide away if some muscle tension is needed to keep them in place. This problem does not exist in the lying position; in the other postures, you may feel things like the hands are slowly sliding to the sides and even hanging alongside, or that the head kind of drops suddenly, or that a strange discomfort comes from your calves or knees. All this can be prevented by adopting the right posture from the start. Those are signs that some muscles had to be at work to keep the body posture, and obviously, your position changes or feels strange when those muscles relax.

Make sure when sitting that you place your hands upon your lap right in the middle, with their weight fully supported, so that they would not fall off even if the muscles were to disappear. The same thing with the legs, forming a more or less right angle at the knee and with the feet flat on the floor. Ladies may find high heels improper for this procedure, and they may prefer to do it barefoot if they do not have flat footwear at the moment.

As the muscles of the neck loosen, the head will tend to go forward, which is fine, let it go. Some people may complain of painful tension in the neck, which indicates that the muscles are returning to their original length, after many years of unnecessary contracture. Do not force it; just allow the body to place itself in its natural shape. For those who suffer from chronic tension in the neck and shoulders, this would be a kind of "autogenous physiotherapy." The discomfort usually disappears after a few days or weeks of training, as the muscles decontract and stretch back to their optimal length.

Mind Attitude

After assuming the right body position and closing the eyes, the second step is to get into the right mind attitude. You would remember here my description of *passive acceptance*. In the beginning, you may work only with the concept, as the live-experience may escape you for some time. Do not worry; it will come. And you would recognize it when it does.

Perhaps you had a glance of passive acceptance when you got into a pleasant peaceful state looking at the sea, or at the waving branches of a forest. This brief moment of bliss is the subjective correlate of passive acceptance. When you concentrate on the waves or whatever, accepting your perception as it is with no judgment or critique, you are getting into passive acceptance.

Another way of approaching passive acceptance is by combining the two common attitudes toward mental activity, which are as follows:

1. Accepting whatever comes to mind that seems interesting or positive, and

2. Rejecting those perceptions, ideas, feelings, and so on that seem uninteresting or negative.

The right mind attitude for meditation is neither of those, but you may approach it by combining both. You develop this third attitude by accepting whatever comes to mind, as if you were interested in it, but with no interest whatsoever in it, without rejecting it. It is easy; do not force yourself at the beginning to understand it. Just practice the experience.

Passive acceptance can be done by itself, but it is hard to maintain for more than a minute. Serious practitioners of *vipassana* may need several years of intense training with an experienced master to keep the passive-acceptance attitude for long periods.

Passive concentration in a selected focus is much easier, and it is a good way to start. Passive acceptance is present, first for a moment as you get into the right mind attitude, and then latent in the background, to be applied to whatever may disrupt the concentration, either from the external or from the internal world.

Focus of Concentration

Traditionally, it is admitted that we have five body senses: vision, hearing, touch, smell, and taste. This is essential for meditation because those senses are useful to focus your mind. Some meditators concentrate on sounds, like in mantra meditation. Others do it on images, like in mandala meditation. Meditation on touch is most popular, with the widely practiced method of sensing how the air passes through your nostrils. Maybe because of the emphasis on fasting, so heartily promoted by yogis, smell and taste are seldom used as focus for meditation. Whatever the traditional reason is, I would much appreciate if someone, perhaps a tantric practitioner, could bring to my attention some practice related to those two forgotten senses.

In fact, the five traditional senses are not the only senses we have. There are more body senses, of which at least three would be of interest for meditators: the vestibular sense, the proprioceptive sense, and the interoceptive sense.

The vestibular sense keeps track of the position of the body and body parts in the space and is in charge, among other things, of keeping the equilibrium. Its training is essential in dancing and in martial arts. The vestibular sense, together with the proprioceptive sense, is the focus of the moving meditations, like tai chi and the Sufi Sema.

The proprioceptive sense works in close cooperation with the vestibular sense and is in charge of detecting the activity of the body and perceiving signals such as muscle tension, body temperature, and the like. It is much the focus of the asana practice of hatha-yoga.

To complete the somatosensory system, we have the interoceptive sense, which perceives the visceral activity generated by the autonomic nervous system, such as gut contractions and vascular dilatation.

The basic technique in autogenics is proprioceptive - interoceptive meditation, that is, passive concentration on somatic sensations spontaneously originated by the own body.

The initial version of autogenic training consisted of six concentration exercises that focus receptive attention on different sensations on different parts of the body. Somatosensory meditation in Autogenics 3.0 follows a smoother sequence of ten exercises, learned one after the other and progressively incorporated into the practice. The sequence begins with passive concentration on mass and heaviness, follows with passive concentration on inner body temperature, on the movement of the heart, on the contact of the skin of the forehead with the atmosphere, and in the respiration process.

Dual Concentration

All types of meditation concentrate on a single focus. So does autogenics, with a novelty called "dual concentration." The focus of concentration in basic autogenics is the experience of the physical sensations coming from the body, but the attention to this experience is paid by two different channels at the same time.

One channel is mental contact with the body, that is, concentration on the direct perception of the selected sensation (heaviness, warmth, etc.). The other channel is indirect and consists in the mental verbalization of the experience, like "my arm is heavy" or "my arm is warm."

Verbalization does not express a wish nor a command but is the verbal rendering of an actual live-experience. (Mental verbalization is appropriate; no need to say the autogenic formula aloud, just repeat it mentally.)

Schultz started dual concentration in the 1930s following a clinical hunch. We have to admire his intuition, as we know now that dual concentration has a solid neuroscientific backing (see p. 66 and following). Autogenics is the only meditation method that specifically trains both sides of the brain and enhances interhemispheric communication.[65]

To put an example, you could well imagine a house without saying anything, and, probably, you could say the word "house" without forming any clear image of a house in your mind, but the experience would be more complete if you combine both representations (see the image in p.67). Studies on brain-hemispheric cognitive specialization show that, for a right-handed person, the picture part is the responsibility of the right hemisphere, whereas the word part is the responsibility of the left hemisphere. As both sides of the brain are interconnected by the corpus callosum, the different ways of coding the information are also interconnected.

Dual concentration in autogenics allows for a complete experience of body sensations, enhances the coherence of information on both sides of the brain, and facilitates the correction of functional interhemispheric disconnection.[66]

How to Handle Distractions?

If you got so far the impression that meditation consists of getting your attention fixed unwaveringly on something, you got only part of it. Your attention will waver, and handling distractions forms part of your training. To start with, consider the six different levels or grades of right concentration (the number increases as the proportion of distraction increases):

1. Total absorption on the focus.
2. Dim awareness of something coming to your mind; you are still in focus.
3. Your attention begins to divide itself between the focus and something else; you realize it and center yourself right away into the focus (so you go back to level 2).
4. Your attention gets hooked into something, and you lose the focus; you realize it, leave the distraction, and come right away to the focus (so you come back to level 3).
5. You begin to get lost into daydreaming or falling asleep; you realize it, you renounce to the distraction, you leave it, and you come back to the focus (you may spend some time on level 4 before you get back to level 3).
6. You get lost into daydreaming of fall asleep. You better finish the exercise, read the whole chapter once more, and try again from the beginning.

Level 2 is the optimal state during basic autogenic training; it blends passive acceptance and passive concentration and opens the ground to advanced autogenics, such as autogenic analysis and feeling meditation, in which the focus is dynamic and passive concentration fuses with passive acceptance.

The level 1 is perfect right concentration. If you are able to maintain your attention at level 1 frequently, by long intervals, and you like it, you may consider leaving autogenics and training yourself in Jahna meditation.[67]

It does not matter how many times you find yourself in levels 3 to 5 during your practice, in a few weeks, you will find yourself most of the time in level 2. But you have to do it seriously, with energetic decision[68] and unbending intent.[69]

The Training Experience

Now and then, a student tells me that he or she gets distracted too much or that he or she can't concentrate at all and feels discouraged. The first thing I say at this point is to change "I can't" by "I find it difficult."

Now that we agree that the exercise is difficult, I inquire about his or her favorite sport. If it is something like skiing, skating, sailing, riding, or surfing, this is very good, as I know he or she has the live-experience he needs, which I call the "training experience." If we cannot find any particular sport to use as an example, it does not matter; I keep looking for the "training experience," which he or she may have got, let's say, learning to drive a car.

Next, I ask him or her to remember how he or she felt like when he or she was learning to…skate, sailing…whatever it was, and what happened as he or she kept practicing. This is the training experience: any technique feels impossible if you do not know how to do it; once you know, it is difficult and, if you keep practicing, becomes as easy as walking.

You are doing the technique right from instant zero, only you are doing it at the level that corresponds to your training stage. The training experience is a continuum, from "impossible" to mastery; there is not a question of getting discouraged or of "trying harder," but of doing it at the level you are. Do your best and do not expect better.

To progress through the training experience, you need *unbending intent*, the helpful mental attitude that Castañeda defines as "Extremely well-defined purpose, not countermanded by any conflicting interests or desires." Or, if you prefer the advice of a Buddhist master, *energetic decision,* Sogyal Rimpoche translation of *Nge Jung* from Tibetan (literal translation "definite emergence"). Energetic decision is complementary of unbending intent and consists in the *ultimate decision of total renouncing of distractions and of not having the slightest interest in anything that gets in the way of concentration.*

Standard Termination of the Exercise

Autogenics may be the only meditation method that has a clear procedure to finish the meditation exercise. The cancellation process comes from the early times of autogenics and intends to mark a sharp distinction between the autogenic state and the regular waking state.

Schultz introduced the cancellation procedure after observing than some trainees experienced a slight dozing or dizzy state for a few minutes after training. Luthe noted that the cancellation procedure ends effectively the autogenic discharges that may be present during the concentration exercises, which could otherwise persist for some time afterward.

The cancellation procedure switches passive concentration into purposeful, active concentration and counteracts several components of the autogenic state. After you decide it is time to finish the exercise, proceed to the cancellation in three steps:

1. Take a purposeful deep breath and let your air out forcefully. In this way, you get voluntary control of your breathing and interrupt its automatic regulation during the autogenic state.
2. Clench your fists, bend your arms and legs, and extend them several times as if you were stretching after a long sleep. You are purposefully tensing your muscles and thus counteracting the muscle-relaxing effect of the autogenic state.
3. Open your eyes. Look around and blink several times. Get out of your inner world and back into the surrounding external world.

If you feel all right, that is it. If you feel a little dozy, repeat the procedure. The cancellation procedure is an easy and effective way to break the autogenic state and come back right away to the normal waking state. You may feel that you do not need it, but I advise you to keep doing it, at least until you are completely free from autogenic discharges.

The anxiolytic effects of the autogenic state would remain anyway for about an hour, something useful to know if you are facing a stressful task, such as public speaking or taking an exam.

7.

SOMATOSENSORY MEDITATION

Basic autogenics begins by getting in touch with your body by somatosensory meditation. Somatosensory means the perception of the activity of your body. There is no question of visualizing, imagining, or memorizing parts of the body, but of getting in direct contact with the experience of the autogenous physical sensations. The senses used to focalize the attention are the proprioceptive and the interoceptive senses. Direct experience of the body leads to knowledge and acceptance of your physical self, which is the first step toward the knowledge and acceptance of your whole self.

The passive concentration in the autogenous physical sensations is always done by dual concentration, which means that you combine *mental contact* (the awareness of the sensations coming from a part of the body) with the *autogenic formula* (the mental verbalization of the sensorial experience).

There are ten somatosensory exercises:

1. Perception of mass = heaviness in extremities
2. Thermogenesis in extremities
3. Thermogenesis in neck and shoulders
4. Thermogenesis in the throat
5. Thermogenesis in the chest
6. Perception of the heart = heart rhythm
7. Thermogenesis in upper abdomen
8. Thermogenesis in lower abdomen
9. Forehead contact with the air
10. Awareness of respiration = autogenous breathing

1. The Experience of Body Mass

Unless you are left handed, you begin this exercise by getting in mental contact with your right arm. If you are left handed, follow the instructions just changing "right" by "left."

We use the right arm for so many different things and so often that our brain has an excellent relationship with it. So, it is the easiest part of the body to begin the experience of mental contact. Once you are well accommodated in your training posture (step one), close your eyes and do nothing. Take a few seconds to set your mind in the "passive-acceptance attitude" (step two).

Now sense how the right arm feels like. There are a lot of nerve fibers coming from each little cell to your brain, so it is easy to receive all this information. You do not have to do anything; just allow yourself to feel all the sensations coming from your arm. You would sense the massif, solid, thick, sturdy quality of your right arm. This is getting in mental contact with your right arm. If the mass of your arm feels a bit strange to you, you may get some help been mindful of a most basic property of mass: its weight. Coming from old French, there is the expression *avoir du pois*, meaning having weight, which was applied to the merchandises that were priced, not by its volume, like fuel, nor by its number, like eggs, but according to its weight, like potatoes.

The notion of weight is interesting. It refers to the force of attraction between two masses, the well-known Newtonian law of gravity. The subjective perception of weight reveals your ability to perceive the force of gravity in action. Your arm will still feel heavy if you were on the moon; only less so, because the moon has less mass than the earth and therefore its force of gravity is lesser. I wonder how it would be like to do this exercise in a gravity-free point in space, a question that could be answered by the NASA astronauts who practice autogenic training.[70]

Do not concentrate on the idea of the arm or try to visualize the arm or anything like that. Go beyond the concept of "arm," get to the live-experience of the arm. This is mental contact with the arm. At the same time, repeat in your mind the words "my right arm is heavy,"[71] which is true. While you concentrate on the truthfulness of the words, you feel the heaviness of the arm. In this way, you are connecting words with a live-experience. This is dual concentration, the autogenic way of training brain interhemispheric connections.

Remember that this is passive concentration; it does not matter if you think that the arm is not as heavy as you expected, or that it is too heavy, or that you could rather call "jitters" or anything else but weight the sensations you are getting. Passive concentration means that you are concentrating on something you know true, and do not care about the results. Accept whatever you happen to feel as what you were exactly supposed to feel, and that is passive concentration. If you are expecting or demanding a particular result, this would be active concentration, that is, concentrating on something to get a particular result and checking if the willed result appears or not. This is fine for most normal life activities, but it is out of the question in meditation. Active efforts to force oneself to feel heaviness was a common pitfall in Autogenics 1.0. Luthe calculated that about one in ten trainees never get the sensation of heaviness, even if the physiological correlates of the autogenic state—decreased skin conductance, lowering pulse rate, and decreased muscle tonus—took place all the same.

If you come to think of it, natural attention is good to detect changes but not so good to make you aware of a continuously stable information. That is why you would quickly notice heaviness is you hang an iron from your arm, but it may take some training to become aware of the unconscious perception of the stable weight that you perceive all the time without notice.

In the beginning, the time of concentration should not exceed ten minutes, even less. Mastery of autogenics does not come from over endurance of a single sitting but from the repetition of short correct exercises. The usual pattern of practice is three times every day. The frequency of training is more important that the duration of every single exercise. It may take from one session to several days to get used to mental contact with your right arm.

Once you feel confident with heaviness in the right arm, you proceed to switch your attention to the left arm.

Remember, this is passive concentration, meaning that you are concentrating on something that is true, but you do not expect, demand, or attempt to force any particular result. If you feel that the heaviness of the right arm persists as you are getting into mental contract with the left arm, this is all right. Shifting attention, particularly at the beginning of training, does often work like unsticking something viscose slowly from the right arm to the left arm, and very rarely as if it were an on-off switch. As you shift the mental contact from arm to arm, you appropriately change the formula to "my left arm is heavy."

After a while, you would sense both arms alike, which is the moment to proceed to the next step, expanding your attention to both arms and coupling the mental contact with the corresponding new formula "my arms are heavy." Take your time to feel confident with each step; don't rush it. It may take from one try to a few days of training. This does not really matter; the question is to feel comfortable with the routine.

Then you leave the arms as they are, and transfer your attention to the right leg, from the hip to the tip of the toes. Mental contact with the leg is usually a bit less intense than with the arms, but it does not matter; keep your passive acceptance and proceed with passive concentration on the mass and heaviness of the right leg, coupled with the mental repetition of the corresponding formula "my right leg is heavy." As soon as you feel confident with this new step, you may proceed to the left leg and after a while amplify your concentration to both legs, as you did with the arms. At each step, you couple the mental contact with the corresponding formula: "my left leg is heavy," then "my legs are heavy." Finally, you expand your concentration to both arms and legs and couple the mental contact with the corresponding new formula "my arms and legs are heavy."

The whole sequence—"my right arm is heavy"—"my left arm is heavy"—"my arms are heavy"—"my right leg is heavy"—"my left leg is heavy"—"my legs are heavy"—"my arms and legs are heavy"—shall take about twenty minutes. Do not set an alarm clock or ask somebody to warn you when the time has lapsed. Calculate the twenty minutes by intuition; you'll be surprised how exact you get on intuitive timing with practice. Do practice three times a day, twenty minutes each time, at least for a week before you go to the second exercise. Do not overdue the time, even if you feel very comfortable and wish to stay longer. On the reverse, if you feel twenty minutes is too long, you may reduce it. Stay at least ten minutes.

After practicing the contact with the sensation of heaviness for at least one week, we may say that you are fully conscious of your physical reality through the awareness of the interaction between your body mass and the mass of the earth. You also have been moving your attention at your will from limb to limb and expanding it to attend several limbs at the same time. This means that you are managing your attention, rather than allowing it to be captured by any haphazard event. Now you are ready for the second step on body awareness: the perception of thermogenesis.

2. The Experience of Thermogenesis in Extremities

As you know, your body tries to keep its internal temperature around 36.5 degrees Celsius (about 98 degrees Fahrenheit). This is an active process called thermogenesis (Latin for heat production), which requires some kind of fuel to produce the necessary energy. At difference to other body functions, there is not a central organ responsible for thermogenesis, a process that takes place in each one of your living cells. What we have is a central thermostat, located in the hypothalamus, which activates or deactivates thermogenic body processes. The hypothalamic set point may vary under certain conditions, such as when the fight against a microbial infection requires increased metabolic activity to activate the defenses. There is a rare illness, malignant hyperthermia, produced by hypothalamic lesions. On the other hand, lack of nutrients, such as in severe malnutrition, may produce hypothermia to spare energy. In the times before home heating was generalized, people needed to eat more in winter than in summer, just to provide this extra fuel. Physical exercise increases muscle metabolism and thus increase body heat. Shivering, an automatic involuntary response, increases muscle metabolism and thus heat production.

Thermogenesis is a sign of life. Corpses are cold because they no longer can perform this function; they keep the properties of mass and heaviness, like any other inanimate object, but they are not alive. Thermogenesis is produced by the metabolism of body nutrients in each living cell, which is easy if the exterior temperature is around twenty-two degrees Celsius, but demands more and more effort as temperature decreases. Decreased blood supply to the body surface is a protective mechanism to reduce heat loss and keep the internal temperature constant. The fingers, the nose, and the ears are expendable body parts, in comparison with the vital organs—the heart, the lungs, the liver, the kidneys, and the brain. If the internal temperature falls below thirty-five degrees, we get into a dangerous condition called hypothermia, which may end in death if the body fails to produce heat faster than it loses it.

The notion of inner- versus surface- body temperature is very relevant to this practice. The specialized sensors in the skin feel the difference between your body temperature and the external temperature and are thus responsible for the sensations of cold and warm. They are very active, as the frequent changes in environmental temperature attract your attention continuously. Other sensors distributed in the connective tissue specialize in perceiving changes in your inner temperature. As this is usually constant, you are aware of their function in rare occasions, such as when you run a fever or when you begin to develop hypothermia.

The purpose of the second autogenic exercise is to train the perception of thermogenesis by developing your awareness of the inner-temperature receptors, disregarding the information provided by the surface receptors.

Before getting into the second exercise, you are to achieve mastery of the first. You are to find it easy to transfer your attention from the right arm to the left arm, then expanding it to both arms, then moving it to the right leg, then to the left leg, then expanding attention to both legs, and, finally, expanding it to arms and legs. After doing this three times a day for at least a week, you may now easily feel the mass and heaviness of arms and legs. If you do not, keep practicing until you feel confident; there is no hurry.

You start the second exercise by resuming the training position and getting into the appropriate mental attitude, as you were doing all previous days. Then skip the usual routine of moving your attention from limb to limb, get into mental contact with arms and legs directly and begin with the last step of the first exercise, "my arms and legs are heavy." If you find this difficult, you may go through the whole routine, but train yourself to begin just with the last step of the heaviness exercise; otherwise, the whole thing would take too much time. We would do the same simplification with the second exercise later on, before going into the third, but now let us train in thermogenesis gradually.

After getting in mental contact with heaviness in arms and legs, move back your attention to the right arm and accept the sensation of warmness that comes from the right arm, from inside out. This is not an effort of the imagination but an acceptance of the perception of warmth. It is the very nature of the arm to be warm, because of the thermogenesis capacity of all its cells. You are sensing this inner warmness all the time, only you are not aware of it.

Do not pay attention to the surface of the arm, including the hand. You are getting into mental contact with the inner receptors of heat and sensing the inner temperature of your arm, which shall be around 36.5 degrees Celsius. We call this property "my right arm is warm," which is a simplified wording of the whole live-experience of thermogenesis. We could say, "It is the nature of the living cells of my right arm to engage in an active energetic metabolism that produces a temperature of around 36.5 degrees Celsius continuously," but this will be far too long, so we resume it to "my right arm is warm."

Notice that you are not giving an order to your arm to heat up, nor do you imagine the sensation of warmness. You are only putting into words a real live-experience: the right arm produces warmth, and this information continuously reaches your brain, even if you are not usually aware of it.

Depending on the external conditions, your surface receptors may perceive cold in the surface of your arm, particularly in the hand, but this is of no interest to you now (passive acceptance). You are concentrating on something that is true; the right arm is producing warmth from inside out and will continue doing it, no matter whether you are aware of it or not.

Do not practice the concentration too long. Five to ten minutes shall be enough, and then repeat the same routine for a few days, until you feel confident that the dual concentration is working well. After some practice with the right arm, you may switch your concentration to the left arm, changing the formula correspondingly to "my left arm is warm." As it did happen with heaviness, you soon will be able to expand the concentration to both arms, coupling the mental contact to thermogenesis with the formula "my arms are warm." After a few days, you would add mental contact with to the right leg, and repeat mentally the accompanying formula, "my right leg is warm." Then you proceed to the left leg, "my left leg is warm," then expand to both legs, "my legs are warm," and, finally, "my arms and legs are warm." Make sure that you maintain the dual concentration, that is, mental contact with the sensation of warmth and simultaneous mental repetition of the corresponding formula.

3. The Experience of Neck and Shoulders Thermogenesis

This exercise is a modification of one of the optional exercises of Autogenics 1.0. It was introduced as a standard exercise in Autogenics 3.0 to improve training in thermogenesis meditation because many patients reported that training only with arms and legs was insufficient. The addition of neck and shoulder thermogenesis enhances the thermogenesis experience and increases the sensation of body relaxation, very convenient for people who have chronic tension in the muscles of neck and shoulders. Thermogenesis training is more demanding and takes longer than the old superficial circulatory training, so it is convenient to increase the sequence of thermogenesis exercises.

In this third exercise, you get into mental contact with the region between the muscles in the back of your neck, just below the occipital bone, and in your shoulders. The corresponding mental verbalization (autogenic formula) is "my neck and shoulders are warm."

Before you begin this exercise, you are to be comfortable with the two previous ones and able to do them starting with the experience, first of heaviness and then of warmth in all four limbs. This would normally take two weeks, one per exercise, but this is just an estimate, and some people may take longer. If you think that you do not need so much time, make sure you are not hurrying. There are no advantages in skipping stages. When you are ready, go as usual to the training posture, then to the mental-acceptance attitude, then distribute your attention on arms and legs and repeat mentally the formula "my arms and legs are heavy." After a few minutes, keeping mental contact with arms and legs, switch to the perception of inner warmness, while repeating the formula "my arms and legs are warm." After a few minutes, switch your attention to your neck and shoulders and sense the warmness produced there, from the inside out. The name of this experience is "my neck and shoulders are warm," so repeat this formula mentally to accompany the direct mental contact with the experience of warmness in neck and shoulders. After a few days, you shall be ready to add the next exercise.

4. The Experience of Throat Thermogenesis

After perceiving the warmth in neck and shoulders, just allow your concentration to penetrate frontward in the thickness of the neck, and sense the warmth produced around the throat. In this exercise, you come in mental contact with the entire region that extends from behind the nose to the upper part of the chest, which includes the pharynx, the esophagus, the thyroid, and all the muscles around. We use the word "throat" to designate all this area for simplicity and apply it to the autogenic formula "my throat is warm." Practice for a few days, three times a day, before you get to the next step. Warmness in the throat is easy to perceive, probably because the internal-temperature receptors have been trained previously by the intake of warm and cold food and liquids.

5. The Experience of Chest Thermogenesis

After the throat exercise, it comes naturally the addition of chest thermogenesis meditation, also a novelty of Autogenics 3.0. Leave the throat as it is and expand your concentration downward into the chest, in all its solid thickness, from side to side, from breast to back and from throat to diaphragm. Sense the warmness produced inside of your chest and, at the same time, repeat mentally the new formula "my chest is warm." This exercise leads to the spontaneous perception of the heart movements, facilitating the next exercise. As always, practice for a few days, three times a day, before you get to the next exercise.

6. The Heart Experience

As you are feeling the warmth produced inside of your chest, you may become aware of the persistent pounding of your heart. The nature of the heart is to keep itself in a continuous repetitive contraction-expansion movement so that it can maintain the blood circulating all through the body. You should feel very grateful to your heart for this constant effort.

Usually, you sense your heart only when you are under stress or when you are involved in strong physical exercise, such as running. However, the heart is active all the time, even if you do not sense it. The mental contact with the warmness produced in the thickness of your chest leads easily to the awareness of the heart movements in the state of rest. When this happens, you are ready to proceed to the sixth exercise, the heart experience.

Once you clearly sense the movements of your heart while concentrating in the warmness produced in the chest, you may switch to the meditation on the heart. In previous versions of autogenics, the heart exercise came right after the concentration on inner warmness in arms and legs. In those versions, many people reported difficulty in experiencing the heart, and some maneuvers were devised to facilitate mental contact with the heart. Since the introduction of chest thermogenesis, very few people report now this difficulty, and most agree that the concentration in warmness in the chest spontaneous and easily makes them aware of the heart movements. Once you perceive your heart, you concentrate your attention in two properties clearly apparent: One is that the heart is calm, as you are neither stressed nor doing any physical exercise. The other is that the heart moves and keeps moving because the continuous movement is its nature. The accompanying autogenic formula, "my heart goes calm and natural," is an easy rendering of your heart experience devoid of any possible uncomfortable connotations. "Goes" is better than "beats" because some people associate "beat" to negative experiences, such as palpitations. To be real pure about dual concentration, you may feel more comfortable reducing the formula to "my heart goes natural." This reduced formula aptly verbalizes the experience of passive concentration on the naturally continuous movement of the heart, without any other extra connotations.

7. The Experience of Upper-Abdominal Thermogenesis

When you feel satisfied with the concentration on the heart movement, go back to the perception of warmth in the chest, and move your attention downward to the upper part of the abdomen. If you know anatomy, you would remember that this space, below the diaphragm and above the umbilicus, contains the stomach and other important organs, such as the spleen, the pancreas, and the liver. But there is no need to know all that; don't try to remember or imagine what is in the upper part of the abdomen, only move your attention there from inside the chest and allow yourself to sense the warmness that is produced in the upper part of your belly.

The proper name of this region is the "midriff," but this word may not be close enough to your everyday experience. You may designate this area by the name of "stomach," which is a convenient name for this region if you do not care about the anatomy textbook. The autogenic formula corresponding to the experience could be "my stomach is warm" or "my upper abdomen is warm" as you prefer.

In previous versions of autogenics, there was much emphasis on locating the solar plexus, a sensitive spot at the transition from the thorax to the pit of the stomach, between the twelfth thoracic and the first lumbar vertebrae. It is all right if you sense it; it is also fine if you wish to place your mental contact in the solar plexus and repeat the old formula (Autogenics 2.0 and 1.0) "my solar plexus is warm." Only expand your awareness to all the surrounding area. When you feel confident about your concentration in the upper-abdominal region, which may take, as usual, from a few days to a whole week, you may continue to the next step.

8. The Experience of Lower-Abdominal Thermogenesis

Move your attention downward to the lower-abdominal region. There, in the space between your navel and your pelvis, you concentrate on sensing the warmness produced in this region from inside outward, coupling the mental contact with the formula "my lower abdomen is warm."[72] If you sense deep inside an inner spot about three fingers below the navel, you are probably getting in mental contact with the Hara region described in the Japanese Zen tradition. You may sense that your attention is being drawn to this point, which is all right; only keep it expanding toward the whole lower-belly region.

What you are doing is interoceptive meditation by dual concentration, that is, mental contact with the warmness produced by the inner abdomen coupled with mental repetition of the formula that says what is going on. Do not confuse it with "body scan" or another form of imaginary visualization of the interior of your body. Do not look for shortcuts, be confident, you do perceive the inner warmness all the time; it is only a matter of recognizing it, of getting aware of something that is always present but never noticed. It is a question of attention training, not of willpower or of imagination.

9. The Forehead-Skin-Temperature Experience

All along, you have been moving your attention from a part of the body to another and from a sensation to another. You have been training your attention to change from place to place at your command, as easily as you would move your pointing finger. Now, as the final practice of mental contact, you would take your attention out of the depth of your belly and move it to the surface of your forehead, in the area where the skin touches the air around you. If you are in a comfortable place and not in the tropics, the chances are that the air touching your forehead skin would be anywhere between eighteen degrees Celsius and twenty-two degrees Celsius, which is a difference of around fourteen degrees Celsius to eighteen degrees Celsius with the temperature inside of your forehead. This is quite a bit of difference, and we call the perception of this difference "my forehead is fresh." The series of mental-contact exercises ends with your concentration in the external sensors of temperature in the forehead's skin. As always, this is passive concentration; you sense the contact of the surrounding air with the skin of the forehead, which is cooler than the inner warmness of the forehead, and you accept anything that you might sense.

10. The Experience of Breathing

Breathing is part of respiration. Unless you are locked in an airtight chamber, the air you are breathing comes in from the most remote confines of the universe and then goes out to infinite distances. You share your air with all living beings, including plants. Once inside of your body the air gets into the minutest cell and comes out from there back into the universe. You may realize that the whole universe participates in your respiration and that your breathing is part of an infinite process that involves all living beings.

We do not know whom or what is in charge of this infinite process, or perhaps nobody cares, and the infinite process of respiration minds itself all by itself. In any event, we would put our concentration in the respiration process, without mental contact with any specific body part. This is the only basic autogenic exercise without mental contact with a part of the body. This is why it comes at the end of the somatosensory series.

According to the dual-concentration principle, we need a phrase for this live-experience, the exact rendering of which would be something like "The universal process of getting air in and out of all living beings takes care of my respiration with no need of any intervention on my part." As the exact formula is a bit cumbersome, please replace it by the shorter formula "it breathes me," where the impersonal pronoun "it" stands for the universal principle of respiration and "breathes me" for "takes care of my respiration with no need of any intervention on my part."

Remember, there is no mental contact. Do not check your nose to sense the air going through it, or your ribs or your diaphragm. Just allow the respiratory process to take care of itself, without any interference from your part.

You may take control of your breathing any time you want, but why would you do it? Just allow breathing to proceed on its own, as you allow the air that comes in to go to every little cell.

Keep your concentration on the experience of breathing and in the universal principle that breaths for you. This universal principle has been around long before your parents were born. It is behind the respiration of all living beings. It has been breathing you since you were born. If you have any concerns, remember the concept of "passive acceptance" and then handle the control of your breathing to the universal respiration principle.

8.

FEELING MEDITATION

After getting used to sensing the body, you are ready for the second level of autogenics: feeling the emotions or, better said, feeling the feelings. In my classification of methods of meditation,[73] this is a dynamic meditation, because the emotions change as you allow them to transform themselves into feelings. Somatosensory meditation, which you just learned in the previous chapters, is a static meditation because there is a constant focus in the stable proprioceptive or interoceptive experience.

The body mass, and hence the weight, does not change during the training exercise; the temperature and the heart frequency may change a little bit, but, for all practical purposes, the focus of concentration is static. When you are doing the somatosensory exercises, you move your attention from a sensation to the next, but on each occasion you are focusing your concentration on an experience that does not change. You could say that breathing is somewhat dynamic because there is an expanding-contracting experience, and you would be right. I do still classify breathing meditation as static because the repetitive and monotonous nature of breathing does not have the fluid quality that feelings and other mental dynamics have. Because of this intermediate condition, and also because it is the only exercise of the somatosensory series without mental contact with a body part, I place breathing meditation at the end of this series. The almost-dynamic quality of breathing, together with the absence of mental contact, makes this last exercise somewhat different from the others, and an appropriate transition to the dynamic meditations.

Feeling meditation begins by allowing the transformation of emotions into feelings. Continues by letting the feelings evolve without interference into the many varieties of the feeling experience, with all its associations, combinations, and shades of nuance and intensity. And finishes when the emotions have completely lost their compelling quality, and the feelings leave the information they intended to deliver from the very beginning.

From Emotions to Feelings Most academic textbooks of psychology treat the words "emotion" and "feeling" as if they were interchangeable, allowing only for the subtle difference that in emotions the physiological experience predominates, while in feelings the subjective experience prevails. Another less-avowed difference is that "emotion" sounds more scientific, whereas feeling has a touch of the poetic and hence an unscientific connotation.[74] In fact, emotion, feeling, and affect are just words that we apply to subjective live-experiences that are quite real.

Following the principle of the mug metaphor formulated in chapter 3, once you live the experience, you may attach it to a word and then search for a conceptual definition of the word. For this purpose, it is useful to look for the etymological roots, as this will give you some inkling into the live-experience your ancestors named with this particular word.

Emotion comes from the Latin *ex-movere*, literally "to move from outside," an expression that fits well with the compelling force of emotions and with the corresponding impression that they are somewhat outside of your control. This is likely the reason why emotions have such a bad name; your caring elders probably admonished you since childhood to "not allow yourself to be carried away by your emotions." The advice is good, but the methods taught by traditional education to carry it out are usually wrong.

The first mistake of the traditional approach is to despise emotions and emotional people, warn against their dangers, and consider that they are poor guides to make decisions. In reverse, it is customary to praise the ability to block, avoid, or ignore emotional experience. This widespread first mistake misses the evolutionary purpose of the emotional-feeling process.

When the early mammalians developed the second brain on earth, what we now call the limbic system, the automatic behavioral responses of the reptiles became more purposeful and sophisticated. The new brain was better able to integrate the perception of the environment and the blind instructions for survival and reproduction coming from the diencephalon, and therefore the early mammals were better able to devise clever plans for surviving and thriving (you may review chapter 5 if you wish). At this point in evolution, emotions are intermediate states between blind hypothalamic reactions and full awareness of the causes and purposes of life's circumstances.

As the limbic system processes the emotion, it becomes an increasingly subjective experience, which then we call feeling. *Emotions are the unconscious awareness of an automatic disposition to act in a particular way upon a particular circumstance for a particular purpose beneficial for survival.* They are the departure point of a process that transforms them into feelings. Of course, there is a fine gradient from the raw unconscious emotion to the fully developed conscious feeling. Most of the time, the emotional–feeling experience is an intermediate state blending urge to act and conscious awareness of circumstances.

The second big mistake of the traditional approach is to classify emotions and feelings as "good" or "bad" or as "positive or negative." It is true that you may like some emotions-feelings and dislike others, but all are useful and carry relevant information. *There are no "destructive emotions," only destructive ways to handle emotions.*

Emotion and feeling are not separate phenomena; they are extremes of a continuous process of increasing awareness and decreasing urge to act. The neurobiological basis of this process is in the limbic system. The neuronal emotional-feeling process begins as an activation of the amygdala, which extends through the cingulate cortex and ends in the prefrontal cortex. Emotions, the beginning of this process, start as unconscious awareness of the automatic urge to act coming from the diencephalon, and, as this impulse is processed through the limbic system, they become more and more conscious, ending up in the purely subjective experience of a fully evolved feeling.

It does not matter if you like the feeling experience or not; all that matters is that, at the end of it, you are able to understand the information provided by the feeling and use this information to turn circumstances into your benefit. When I say, "understand the information provided by the feeling," "understand" does not mean explaining, reasoning, or looking for what caused the feeling, but rather the awareness of the significance of the live-experience of the feeling. Let us use the expression "feeling the feeling," to avoid the confusion that "understanding the feeling" may create.[75]

Feelings Are Opinions

In academic psychology, emotions and feelings belong to the category of "the irrational" and are clearly differentiated from the more elevated cognitive functions. In chapter 5, you read how the diencephalon, our first brain, regulates the vegetative body functions and the five behaviors essential for survival and reproduction (eating, drinking, sleeping, fight-flight, and raw sex). We could say that the diencephalon makes decisions necessary for maintaining body homeostasis, such as pumping the right amount of blood to keep every cell well nourished, and about behaviors good for survival, such as eating, running out of danger, or falling asleep. However, I am not sure if we can say that the diencephalon makes opinions.[76] *Opinions imply an evaluation of the circumstances and a plan of action to modify them in your benefit.*

Neuroscience and cognitive psychology have quite agreed that thinking is a function of our third brain, the neocortex, also in charge of final processing of sensorial inputs and the control of body movements. Your conscious opinions come from your reasoning, which is the work of your frontal lobes. They integrate the information coming from your sensorial cortex, they form models of the future consequences of alternate behaviors, they decide the best action plan, they send the appropriate instructions to your motor cortex, and *voilà*, you are behaving in the most reasonable way.

Meanwhile, the second brain, your limbic system, also called the inner brain because it is inside the neocortex, does not have any inkling of what is going on. It has no direct connection with the external world, so it has to make do with whatever the neocortex feeds it. There is no way it can differentiate between an accurate rendering of the environment and the memories, fantasies, and imaginations made by the powerful neocortex. For the limbic system, it is the same if a ferocious rhinoceros charges at you that if you are watching a Godzilla movie. It takes some time for the neocortex to learn how to add little tags to the information it sends downward, such as "this is a movie," "this is a fantasy," and "this is a dream." I hope you got all your tags right when you were little. I know many grown-ups who react to their fancies and fears as if they were really happening. In any case, the emotional reaction would still occur, even if tempered by the extra information of the tags.

The limbic system, situated between the neocortex and the diencephalon, gets information from one side about whatever the neocortex thinks is happening and from the other side about whatever the diencephalon senses as relevant for survival and reproduction. Diencephalic information to the limbic system comes directly from the thalamus bypassing the cortex,[77] and there are probably more unchartered hypothalamic-limbic connections.[78] After integrating all this information, the limbic system would make what I say is an opinion, that is, an evaluation of circumstances and a plan of action to modify them on your benefit. The limbic opinion begins as an unconscious emotion and evolves until it becomes a fully developed feeling. Only when the limbic opinion becomes fully conscious, it can be further processed and integrated with the cognitive opinions.

To give a few examples, fear is the limbic opinion that something dangerous is about to happen; anger, that something is hindering your life or impinging in your territory and has to be eliminated; sadness, that you lost something beneficial; love, that something very beneficial exists; attachment, that you want to keep possesion of something beneficial; and so on.

Limbic Processing of the Emotion-Feeling Continuum

If an opinion requires some previous processing, pure emotions are not really opinions, as they are too close to hypothalamic decisions and you feel them as vegetative reactions with an automatic bodily urge to act. Much of the old theorizing about emotions and feelings was made on raw emotions, which explains why so little progress has been achieved.[79]

The important point of my new approach is that raw emotions are processed by the limbic system and progressively transformed in conscious subjective feelings. Feelings do not impose an urge to act, and they can associate, combine, and modify each other. The practical core of my theory of limbic processing is that emotion cannot be reasoned before it fully transforms itself into a complete feeling. Then, reason and emotion do not compete or oppose each other but cooperate as two sequential modes of information processing and decision making.

From the evolutionary perspective, the apparition of the third brain makes a lot of sense, as it continues the work of adaptation from where the second brain was able to guide it.[80] Feelings are limbic opinions that the neocortex can process as to the details of how, when, where, and if they are to be implemented.[81] It follows that the important life decisions are made by the limbic system and that the powerful cortex is just a diligent servant that works the details of doing it. In neurobiological terms, the limbic processing begins when the raw diencephalic discharges on the service of survival activate the amygdala, continue through the cingulate cortex, and end up in the orbitofrontal cortex, from where the processes of reasoning begin.

Blocking of the Emotion-Feeling Processing

If everything proceeds smoothly, the hypothalamic impulses and the emotional memories stored in the hippocampus reach the amygdala and continue unhindered through the cingulate cortex, to end in the orbitofrontal cortex. I call this process feeling the emotion, or feeling the feeling, which is the same that allowing the feeling to develop from the emotion. This process gives feelings their dynamic quality, a fluid subjective experience mirroring the flowing of neuronal impulses along the limbic system. However, this process can be slowed, interfered with, or blocked. Most people try to avoid in variable ways the feeling process, because of the two fundamental mistakes of traditional education explained above. Also, it is quite natural to refuse living an unpleasant experience, such as sorrow, fear, and anger. Less common, but also possible, is the blocking of pleasurable feelings, such as love or joy.

On occasions, feelings might be of such a tremendous intensity, or they may come at such an early time in life, that the limbic system is not capable or mature enough to handle them. Nature has supplied humans with a unique prohomeostatic mechanism to transfer overflowing strong feelings out of the feeling- channel into the sensorimotor system: the natural reflex of crying. Crying discharges painful tensions without harm, through the activation of complex muscular systems and parasympathetic functions. Luthe discovered early the powerful therapeutic effect of crying and described forced crying as the first of his methods of autogenic neutralization.[82]

As you progress in feeling meditation, you will discover that the pleasant or unpleasant quality of feelings disappears after you feel the feeling. This is the reason why pleasurable feelings, which are usually felt willingly, last shorter than the unpleasant ones, which are often blocked.

There are many strategies to block the feeling process, and all involve some activity different from allowing the feeling to evolve. The blocking strategies may overlap and confound themselves with the effects of diverted feelings. Some of the most common strategies to deflect feelings are as follows:

- Trying to convince yourself that you should not feel that way. This is a bad policy, because, on top of the bad feeling, you feel guilty and stupid.

- Trying to convince yourself that the feelings have no reason to be, which is not that bad, although usually ineffective.

- Searching for reasons and explanations (often wrong) of why you feel that way.

- Entering into arguments with yourself about why you did this, why somebody else did that, and so on.

- Start chatting about anything with anybody, or even with yourself.

- Moving nervously along, looking for any distracting activity such as going to the movies and putting on the TV or the music.

There are many other ways to block the emotion-feeling continuum, but you get the point. Check what you do when you experience an unpleasant emotion, and let me know if you find some new trick to add to my list.

In fact, it does not matter which tactics you use. Even if some may seem to work for some time, they all have the same purpose: to distract you from feeling your feeling. And an unfelt feeling will keep coming back; it does not matter how long ago the circumstances that prompted it did disappear.

The pressure of the unfelt blocked feeling may force its diversion to other channels, such as the thinking channel (cortex) or the body channel (diencephalon). There are three possible derivations of unfelt feelings (see image):

1. To the frontal lobe. This diversion causes two groups of symptoms: either a foggy mind, with difficulty in concentrating and forgetfulness, or else repetitive meaningless obsessional thoughts.

2. To the motor- or sensorial-parietal cortex, producing uncoordinated movements and twitching or seemingly purposeful behavior, such as running, shouting, or banging walls.
3. Down to the hypothalamus, disturbing vegetative functions, such as blood pressure, heartbeat, respiration and vigilance.

BLOCKING THE FEELING PROCESS

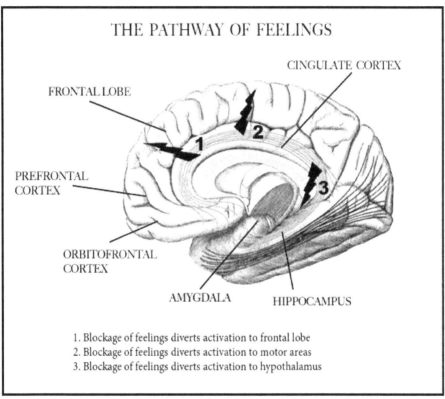

THE PATHWAY OF FEELINGS

CINGULATE CORTEX

FRONTAL LOBE

PREFRONTAL CORTEX

ORBITOFRONTAL CORTEX

AMYGDALA   HIPPOCAMPUS

1. Blockage of feelings diverts activation to frontal lobe
2. Blockage of feelings diverts activation to motor areas
3. Blockage of feelings diverts activation to hypothalamus

Arrows indicate the diversion of limbic impulses away from the cingulate cortex towards other brain areas.

How to Do Feeling Meditation.

You are now into the practical part. To do feeling meditation, you need three previous conditions:

1. Proper training in somatosensory meditation. – You learned that in previous chapters.
2. A conceptual framework for the transformation of emotions into feelings. – You got that in this chapter.
3. Energetic Decision and Unbending Intent. This was in *The Training Experience*, p 86. See also notes 67 and 68.

Now that you are ready, wait until some strong emotion comes along. Any emotion would do, but a strong one is better because it will be easier for you to realize how strongly you oppose the feeling process. Fear is a good one to try, but you may decide other, such as rage or sadness. Do not try to provoke the emotion willfully, be incidental, and take advantage of spontaneous emotions; you would have plenty of opportunities.

Emotions usually come accompanied by body activity, such as muscle tension, restlessness, palpitations, and reddening of the face. Do not pay attention to body sensations. Before you continue, remember *passive acceptance*. If the emotion is strongly unpleasant and you think that you are suffering a lot, apply passive acceptance to suffering, and you would realize that suffering has no value. I do not mean that suffering is no-good, bad, or negative, much less that it is meritorious or worthy. What I mean is that suffering is useless. Suffering does not matter; the only thing that matters is to allow your feeling to evolve.[83]

Your first discovery on how to do feeling meditation is that there is nothing to do. You only have to stop doing what you usually do when an unpleasant feeling comes. Blocking uncomfortable feelings is automatic. Review all your blocking strategies and renounce to them all. It is an easy decision, but you have to take it. Do nothing, accept the feeling, and see what happens. Do not bother to "observe"; you are observing anyway; I mean, you are there, and you feel how your feeling feels. If you know the name of the feeling, you may say it aloud. Not too loud, just verbalize the name soft and short.

Feeling meditation is contra-intuitive. Many treatises on psychology emphasize the importance of "being in touch with your feelings," but none explains how to do it.[84] Even Buddha, in the second chapter of the Satipatthana,[85] commends the "meditation on feelings as feelings" but does not say how to do it. Or perhaps he did, and the instructions got lost in translation. The truth is that when I explained feeling meditation to the yogi master Alejandro Torrealba, he looked at me seriously and said, "this is pure *vipassana*." He was right, as usual. For more than twenty years, he has helped me greatly to wade through the Buddhist writings, and every time I share with him some advanced experience with autogenics, he finds an adequate correspondence within his Tibetan tradition. Feeling meditation is focalized *vipassana*. You do not divert your attention to everything that comes up, as some people may define mindfulness, but you keep your passive concentration on the dynamics of the feeling.

The secret is to notice the blocking strategies. They are completely natural and automatic; they come for the obvious reason that you try to avoid what you do not like.

Feeling meditation seems difficult when, in fact, it is effortless: you have to do nothing. But to do nothing, you have first to accept that you got a feeling, that the feeling is yours, and that you want to own your feeling because it is yours. It does not matter whether you like it. This is passive acceptance. Accept that you do not like the feeling and that you want to block and to avoid it. Accept all this, and do nothing. This is also passive acceptance.

While you do nothing, you will notice that the feeling has a life of its own and it is evolving by itself. Anything you do is only a strategy to block the feeling, so do nothing. Just verbalize the name of the feeling; remember, words are handles. Putting a handle on your live-experience will help you to understand it better later on. Later, not now. When you are feeling the feeling, you are only feeling the feeling, do not allow naming the feeling to be an interference. Keep the verbalization effort to a minimum; if you do not know the name, do not care. It will come; just keep feeling the feeling.

Feeling the feeling may seem impossible the first few times; the experience might frighten you, or you might simply go back to your old habits of blocking the feelings. It does not matter; it is only a question of training. Review the chapter and make sure that your attitudes toward emotions and feelings have changed. Make sure that your reading marks a before and an after. Before, you disliked, despised, and distrusted your feelings; now, you appreciate them, you want to own them, you recognize them as worthwhile achievements of nature, and as the harbingers of useful information. This shift of mind makes all the difference.

I remember the case of a Buddhist nun who came to my office because of severe bouts of depression and anxiety. Quite candidly, I asked her what effect meditation had on her symptoms, and she answered that, since the symptoms began, she could not meditate. After some prodding, we started somatosensory meditation, and, quite spontaneously, she experienced a feeling of anger. She immediately interrupted the meditation, and she explained to me that she should not feel angry, that anger was against her Buddhist beliefs and that she should always feel love and compassion. It took some time to agree that feelings are not voluntary, that they happen as they happen, and that it is only a matter of not allowing them to disturb your meditation. You may force yourself to act kindly because you have (some) voluntary control over your actions, but you cannot force yourself to feel kindness if what you feel is rage. Of course, you want to feel kindness and not rage, but the way to do it is not to fight rage but to allow it to dissolve in meditation.

I share this short vignette with you to show that even devoted and experienced meditators may have a wrong understanding of what a feeling is. The story has a good end; after her first try in feeling meditation, she was quite surprised to notice that her anger slowly faded away. She had been months fighting this rage, getting exhausted in the process, to no avail. Feeling meditation allowed her to transform the feeling into information about her life circumstances, which we could calmly discuss *after* the feeling had run its course.

It does not matter how loud and clear I repeat it, you will only allow passive acceptance of your feelings when you have the actual experience of the feeling fading away, usually after it seems that you cannot stand it any longer. This is normal. After you have done it a few times, you would realize how easy it is, and you will wonder why nobody told you before.

Together with passive acceptance, there is another mental chip to help you in your feeling meditation: curiosity. Wanting to know what happens when you accept your feelings may seem to run counter *passive acceptance*, but do not be picky. You need a reason to embark yourself into feeling meditation, and curiosity is a good one. Of course, there are other reasons, like getting free from unpleasant feeling and liberating the energy wasted in blocking your feelings, but it is convenient to have also a positive reason. Curiosity also means that you want to know the information your limbic system is trying to deliver. You accept the workings of this important part of your brain, and you are interested in its opinion. Those are the main reasons; it is good that you know that the unpleasantness of the bad feelings would disappear, but this is only an ancillary motivation; don't let this be your primary reason.

Sometimes, you may feel like you do not feel anything. This is impossible because there is always a feeling. The limbic system is continuously analyzing everything that comes to it and is always emitting an opinion. When you feel that you do not feel anything, there are three possibilities:

- You are facing a block. Even if you are fully for feeling meditation, you may still block the feeling process automatically. Accept the blocking and then accept the feeling that you do not want to feel.

-   You are feeling confusion. Several feelings are coming together, and you do not know how to sort them out. Some of them may be incompatible, like love and hate (a combination that usually evolves into guilt). Accept all of them together, and then let any one of them evolve.
-   You are feeling void, "I do not understand anything," disbelief, negative wonder, disavowal. This is rare, but it happens. You are getting a feeling related to some very traumatic or contradictory event of your life. Do more basic somatosensory meditation before you continue feeling meditation.

The Sequence of Feeling Meditation

You begin feeling meditation not knowing what is going to happen. Do not make assumptions, just accept whatever feeling comes first and do not interfere with its evolution. Renounce to all your thoughts, explanations, memories, or movements. Keep still, in your favorite meditation posture, accept that all sorts of things are coming to your mind, and keep on the feeling track. It does not matter what memories, images, persons, or whatever come associated with the feeling. Those are only distractions and strategies to prevent you from *feeling the feeling*. Keep on track, give the feeling a name if this is easy, and keep on track.

Let us say that you start with fear, which is the most frequent and easy feeling, in all its variants of anxiety, anguish, preoccupation, foreboding, and the like. In the simplest case, you will notice that, after what seems a horribly unbearable experience, the intensity of the fear decreases, maybe changes into one of its nuances, and finally fades away. Fear is the limbic opinion that something bad is about to happen. After you feel comfortable with this opinion, it is time to think how valuable and useful it may be. Remember that your limbic system opinions are at the level of a pet's opinions. You would not allow your pet to run your life, but I am sure that you are considerate to its opinions. Sometimes, they are accurate and useful; often they are redundant or based on the wrong perception of the circumstances.

Now let us consider the source of feelings. They are always opinions made by your inner brain about how the circumstances can affect you, but how does your inner brain know about the circumstances? It is inside, enveloped by the cortex, with no direct connection to the external world (except for odors) and has to rely on whatever information the cortical sensory areas and the hypothalamus feed on it. Therefore, you will find feelings produced in response to five types of circumstances:

1. Real current-life circumstances happening right now in your external world that may have a direct impact on your well-being. That is, a lion is running at you.
2. Fake or represented circumstances. That is, you are watching a movie of a lion running at you.
3. Imagined possible life circumstances. You are boarding a plane, and you think it may crash. You are to take an exam and you think you may flunk.
4. Memories of past life circumstances. You were persecuted by a lion (well, a furious dog) when you were a child.
5. Vital feelings. A body organ is malfunctioning, and your limbic system makes an opinion about this malfunction. Sorrow may be the first symptoms of pancreatic cancer. Some women feel irritable,

anxious, or sad around menstrual times (I know, this is not a malfunction, but it is a vital feeling anyway). Many men feel despondent after middle age when their testosterone levels fall.

After fear, the most common feeling is probably anger. Because of education and other social pressures, some people develop a great ability *not to* feel angry. If you block anger for a long time, it will overflow the feeling track and disturb other areas of functioning, such as:

(a) the hypothalamus, producing all kinds of psychosomatic disorders, like hypertension;

(b) the motor areas, producing restlessness and chronic contractures; or

(c) the frontal lobes, feeding repetitive, pointless thoughts.

Other blocked feelings would do the same. Repressed fear tends to disturb the digestive tract and to numb the reasoning ability. Repressed sorrow tends to convert into chest pressure and breathing difficulties.

When allowed to follow its natural evolution, no feeling is eternal: all begin, continue, and end. However, it will persist if you block it, forever pressing to overcome the blockade. Even if the circumstances that caused the feeling disappeared many years ago, it would persist in trying to follow its course.

There is a difference between partially blocking a feeling, which is frequent in anxiety, and totally repressing a feeling, which is more common with anger and longing. Partial blocking prevents the feeling from evolving, so that it never gets fully processed, but does not prevent you from being aware of it. Total blocking prevents the feeling to be fully processed, *and* to become conscious. In my clinical experience, the most common entirely repressed feeling, probably even more than rage, is longing for love.

Many people get stuck on feelings of sadness, loneliness, impotence, and depression because they fail to perceive their connection to the need for love. Even finding a name for this feeling may be difficult; one of my patients called it "nobody loves me." He invariably ended his meditation crying, the only safe physical drain provided by nature to overflowing feelings. Once he discovered and neutralized the "nobody loves me" feeling, his chronic depression and unhappiness progressively lifted. Some harmful life dynamics also disappeared, such as excessive alcohol consumption and philandering tendencies. This is interesting, as this change in behavior was not mediated by any rational comprehension or by any effort of will. Both trends faded away as he processed the longing feeling thoroughly; at the same time, he also became able to enjoy the genuine affection of his family and friends.

Full processing requires living the feeling without resistance, with all its nuances and intensities, until you get so used to it that it becomes tedious. When the feeling becomes simply information, you are able to process it further by reasoning and then act appropriately if it responds to actual circumstances, or forget about it if it is an obsolete opinion about past or imagined circumstances.

Never start the process by remembering or inducing a particular emotion purposely. The seed for feeling meditation must be spontaneous and actual. For this reason, you better do it when the need arises, not following a schedule, as you do with somatosensory meditation. Only, if you are not alone or the situation is not appropriate, you may keep a current feeling for later. Some obsolete feelings may be almost continuously present, so they are easy to access at any time. If you get stuck or the unpleasant feeling does not seem to end, overlap your feeling meditation with regular somatosensory meditation.

Often, when a feeling is fading away, another does emerge. Fear may lead to anger, which usually means that you were afraid of your anger. After anger, sadness may appear; sadness may lead to abandonment or to loneliness. Different feelings may mix and conflict in various manners. Anger and sorrow, for instance, often lead to guilt, which usually ends up in remorse and reparation. Self-hate is always a sign of blocking; it usually appears when love mixes with rage, as in pathological grief.

The possibilities are many, although some are more frequent than others. In the next autogenics book 2, *Clinical Autogenics*, there will be further examples and clinical vignettes. By now, do your own work and write down the experience.

Short dictionary of feelings—what your limbic system thinks of your live-experience:

Fear: This situation is dangerous.

Anxiety: Something very bad is about to happen.

Anguish or panic: Something very bad is happening right now.

Sorrow: I lost something or somebody very important.

Guilt: I caused the loss or harm of somebody or something very important to me.

Responsibility: I am the one who must take care or to solve this situation.

Reparation: I must recover, mend, compensate for something important I harmed or destroyed.

Shame: I am quite below the expectations of somebody very important.

Apathy: There is nothing interesting, valuable, or loving in my life.

Sadness: There is nothing interesting, valuable, or loving in my life, and this will not change.

Rage: I must eliminate something or somebody who is impinging in my territory or blocking my way.

Surprise: I am not prepared for this new, unexpected situation.

Longing: I need to be loved.

Frustration: I am trying to get something and it seems that I can't get it.

Impotence: I have been trying to get something, and I give up because I can't get it.

Do you want to complete or comment this short dictionary? Please, do it. Listen to your limbic system, love it as you would love your most favorite pet, let the feeling evolve until is over, and then write your translation into words.

9.

MEDITATION ON FEELINGS

"Meditation on feelings" and "feeling meditation," despite the similitude of names, are two entirely different procedures.

Feeling meditation is dynamic meditation because the focus is on the changing evolution of your emotions. Feeling meditation does enable you to be aware of the spontaneous opinions of your limbic system and to be totally comfortable with your emotions. Fully processed feelings are useful information about real, faked, remembered, or imagined circumstances. Because the unpleasant feelings are blocked more often than the pleasant ones, the feelings that come up for meditation are usually disturbing and unpleasant.

On the other hand, "meditation on feelings" is passive concentration on a predefined feeling, chosen because it is deemed beneficial for your personal development. Meditation on feelings is static meditation because the focus is on the unchanging selected feeling.

Both feeling meditation and meditation on feelings produce important psychological effects, which are opposite, or, better, complementary. Feeling meditation facilitates the processing and deactivation of undesired feelings and follows the neutralization principle.[86] Meditation on feelings increases the presence of feelings that have a constructive influence on your life and follows the ideoplastic principle.[87] In short, you can think of *feeling meditation* as a cleaning process of disturbing emotions, and of *meditation on feelings* as a procedure to increase the power of constructive feelings.

What Are Constructive Feelings?

Emotions are the dim awareness of a tendency to action. As they get more and more conscious, they become the subjective opinion called feeling. In chapter 8, you learned how to facilitate this process following the method of feeling meditation. In that same chapter, I said that there are no destructive emotions, only destructive ways of handling emotions. The most destructive way of handling an emotion is blocking its evolution to feeling.

Blocking emotions is destructive because of:

(1) The limbic impulses are diverted to other areas of the brain, which get thus inappropriately activated.

(2) The blockade of the emotion-feeling process wastes energy needed to adapt to the circumstances.[88]

(3) The information provided by insufficiently processed feelings is blurred or lost.

(4) The action tendency to modify a situation persists time after this situation has ceased to exist.

In this sense, all your feelings are constructive because they all give you information about your circumstances and thus enable you to make the best out of them. As circumstances change, so do the feelings change. It is senseless wanting to change the way you feel when what you need is action to modify your circumstances. Sometimes, you cannot change anything right away; then you may vary your point of view or resort to autoplastic adaptation (change yourself) or heteroplastic adaptation (move to another environment).

In any event, remember the piece of wisdom Roman Emperor Marcus Aurelius learned from Epictetus: "Change what can be changed and accept what cannot be changed." It is also useful to study Buddha's first noble truth: "life is hard."[89] When it rains, it rains. It is silly to complain and to be despondent because of the rain. You better get used to it, find out how not to get soaked, and, the wisest thing, enjoy singing in the rain.[90]

Sages from across the ages have detected a few feelings that seem adequate opinions about the universe. People who hold those feelings on a permanent basis live the healthiest and happiest lives, a fact known by traditional wisdom and demonstrated by recent scientific research. Lifelong feelings of peacefulness, love, empathy, and enjoying the present correlate with quality of life and longevity.[91] Those feelings we may truly call constructive feelings because they are correct limbic opinions about unchanging truths. Feelings about impermanent circumstances are bound to change; constructive feelings are not, so you may hold them on a permanent basis.

Selecting Feelings for Meditation

Meditation on feelings is a general approach. It does not persecute a particular therapeutic aim, it is suitable for universal application, and it is appropriate for anybody wishing to expand her awareness about herself and the universe. Therefore, the feelings selected are the "truly constructive feelings," taught by the old schools of wisdom, singularly by the Greek Stoics and by the Theravada tradition.[92] Meditation on feelings other than the truly constructive ones may be indicated in autogenic modification, a highly individualized method of autogenic therapy, carefully adjusted to the personality and to the clinical stage of each patient. This advanced method of autogenic therapy is discussed in autogenics book 2, *Clinical Autogenics*.

The truly constructive feelings selected for meditation on feelings, in order of difficulty, are calm, existence, zest, and love.

1. Calm

Calm emerges quite naturally during the practice of meditation and constitutes a universal experience, a basic feeling tone common to all meditative practices. It is also the first constructive feeling to come to the awareness of the meditator (de Rivera and Trujillo, 1996, 2010). Some meditators affirm that they had never experienced this feeling before they learned meditation, while others recall similar experiences during spontaneous trance or during casual instances of passive concentration, such as gazing at the sea. Many meditators agree that it's hard to find a precise word to name it in full justice. I have chosen "calm" because it is easy, wide, and close to the live-experience, while others prefer words such as "peace," "relaxation," "tranquility," "equanimity," "serenity," "security," "placidity," "beatitude," and "ataraxy." All those words apply to nuances of the same underlying feeling and reflect preferences of the meditator. For some people "calm" has more physical connotations, "peace" is ampler and more interpersonal, "serenity" and "equanimity" have more the connotation of imperturbability, and so on. You are free to choose the name that best relates to your experience.

Relaxation, besides its familiar meaning of absence of tension, has a technical meaning since Herbert Benson described the *relaxation response,* the typical psychophysiological reaction during passive concentration. The objective physiological components of this response are accompanied by the subjective feeling of relaxation that I have proposed to define as: "An experience in all opposed to anxiety, a pleasant diffuse feeling that everything is all right and nothing bad can possibly happen."

Albeit it may be useful to oppose relaxation and anxiety for description purposes, it is important to realize that relaxation (or calm) is not the mere absence of anxiety; both are feelings on their own right and may even coexist for a short time. If you start the somatosensory autogenic exercise while you are experiencing anxiety or tension, you will notice that the feeling of anxiety seems even stronger at the beginning, only because it is felt better, and that it progressively fades away while calm increases.

You may begin the practice of meditation on calm after a few weeks of training in somatosensory meditation. Once you clearly and consistently experience the feeling of calm during your autogenic training, start recalling it for a few seconds right after terminating the exercise. At this moment, the feeling is very near your consciousness, and it should be easy to recall; minimal effort is involved. It is only a slight recollection of the relaxation experience that you just lived. Often, some physical sensations may accompany the feeling; if there is one that is interesting to you, you may incorporate it in the recall.

2. Existence

Existing is such an extraordinary experience that everything else is only a little detail. It is all right to pay attention to all the details of life if you wish, but always keep in mind that they are only little details. As it happens with calm, there are many words for the feeling of existence. One is "being present," which is often thought of as an act of will or as a cognitive effort. In fact, it is the natural expression of the feeling of existence. Glimpses of *being* may come spontaneously during somatosensory meditation, and more frequently during feeling meditation.

After the experience of strong disturbing feelings, if you persist on the passive-acceptance attitude when the feeling seems unbearable, there is a sudden change to the feeling of existence. Remember that passive acceptance is not giving any appreciation, in favor or against, to anything that comes to mind. This is easy when banal things or light feelings come, but it is much harder when what comes up are strong feelings of desperation, hopelessness, and the like. Yet, the attitude is the same, and you know well how to keep it. The only trick is to remember that you have to maintain the passive-acceptance attitude. See my endnote 83 if you want to find out how I discovered the feeling of existence after going through "point zero," and avoid the mistake of giving value to suffering. Suffering is a feeling like any other and has no particular value whatsoever.

Do not believe that the feelings either of despair or of impending death are permanent. They are not. When the experience cannot get any worse, and you maintain passive acceptance in this "point zero," you would discover the great feeling of existence. When everything is lost, you realize that all you got is life and that this is the most valuable thing. Being aware that you are alive is a magnificent experience, and you can get it only if you do not get distracted by little details. Once you get this feeling, memorize it and recall it often. You may name the feeling "I exist" or "I am" or "I am I." Do not worry by admonitions that you have to renounce your ego; the feeling of "I am" has nothing to do with the ego. It is what is left when you abandon your ego and are still alive.

At some moment in your life, you would have an opportunity, probably only once, to give up the feeling of existence. It is better that you own it very well, or else you would not know how to surrender it to the infinitude. Glimpses of merging with a larger existence may come when you meditate, a feeling usually called "transcendence." This is very good, but do not overdo it, unless you want to become a full-fledged mystic.

3. Zest

Bertrand Russell lists this feeling like one of the most important causes of happiness. It is the feeling of thoroughly enjoying what you do, and you can think of it as a variant of enthusiasm. After realizing existence, it easily comes out that living is action. It does not matter what you do; you are in zest if you do fully immerse in your action. The experience of zest may come in very simple circumstances, as when you enjoy a meal or any other likable activity, provided that you enjoy it fully, without distractions or extraneous thoughts. Living with acceptance of the past and with curiosity for the future is a quality of zest, which entirely counteracts remorse and fear. Being present in what you are doing is an expression of zest and a natural evolution of the feelings of calm and existence.

When you are full of interest and zest for the object of your activity, the magic of mindfulness is effortless. But it is quite impossible if you try to impose mindfulness on yourself as a duty. Evoke the feeling of zest when you go on a walk, not necessarily by a peaceful countryside, and observe with curiosity and without prejudice —with passive acceptance— everything you come along. Look at the trees as if you have never seen one before. Sense the presence of the passersby, notice their faces, their walking, muse yourself about anything they may do. Do not judge; accept everything as it is. And then, suddenly, you may discover that you are enjoying the simplest experience better than the most sophisticated spectacle. Then keep this feeling of zest in your memory, get it back often, and you will enjoy and benefit from what could otherwise be boring circumstances.

Another version of zest is "always do your best." This is the advice given to me by the Toltec *Nagual* Miguel Ruiz. The question is not doing the perfect job, achieving the best result, outperforming everybody, no; doing your best is putting all your being on what you are doing, as you are right then and there. Do not waste energies complaining that you could do better if you were healthier, less tired, or had the adequate tools. *El que hace lo que puede no esta obligado a más*— He who does what he can is not required to do more—says a Spanish proverb. You are not the same all the time; your energies, your abilities, even your body vary all the time. However, if you have zest, you will always do your best. Cultivate the feeling of zest in your meditation, and bring it often to your everyday life, especially when it feels boring or hard.

4. Love

This is the most overused and confusing word for a feeling. Its erotic and romantic connotations in the modern mind are a problem when you want to approach the subject seriously. Yet, *love* is a very simple and straightforward feeling: it is the pleasure at the existence of something. It blends with and develops from the other truly constructive feelings: it is the plenitude of calm, the happiness of existence, the joy of zest. You may love a person, a pet, a plant, your hometown, the sun and the stars, your job, your own existence, the universe all. But the question gets complicated when you go to the practical experience of love.

First, you have to sort out the confusion between loving and being loved. Your first contact with the feeling of love is receptive. If love is the pleasure at the existence of somebody, being loved means that somebody experiences pleasure at your existence. Life was given to you and love was given to you, and the only thing you had to do to receive both was to accept them. You learn the feeling of love by empathy, by experiencing the pleasure of somebody at your existence. This happened. You would not be here had you not been loved dearly at some early point in your life.

Now, if love is such an important question, it makes sense trying to secure it at all costs. You may fear that existing is not enough and then you resort to tricks to get love. Longing for love is one of the most frequent and burdensome blocked feelings uncovered by feeling meditation. The need for love means that you feel that you are not getting enough love or that the love you get is unsatisfactory.

Strangely, the harder you try to be loved, the less love you would get, and the love you get would be less satisfactory. Why is this so? It is easy to understand: if you make an effort to please someone to get his or her love, you are forcing an effect, you are manipulating this person to love you. Even if he or she responds, he or she would not be taking pleasure on your existence, on whom you are, but in what you are doing to please him. In fact, he or she may even dislike you because you are trying to seduce him or her, even if he or she may take advantage of your efforts.

On the other hand, if you behave as you are, somebody would love you, and this would be real love. If you are calm and attentive, behave full of zest, and feel pleasure on the existence of the others, most people would love you. If you want to be loved, just love existence in general and yours in particular; keep calm and always do your best. And above everything else, get free from the "nobody loves me" feeling. Then you would realize how easy it is to love and how much love you receive.

The second question with love is differentiating love from attachment and from possession, which is the most malignant and extreme form of attachment. If you love a flower, you feel pleasure at it; perhaps you may even water it or otherwise care for it. If you need to go often to watch the flower and you miss it when you do not see it, you are attached to it. If you cut the flower and take it home in a vase, you possess it.

Attachment is a natural bond that forms to whom you love. You make it with persons, animals, places, behaviors, or to anything that ever pleased you. It is unavoidable. Attachments develop stronger when other feelings mix with love. Even hate may form strong bonds. Attachments are the base of all social structures; in one way, they give meaning to your life, but in another way, they limit your freedom. The main problems with attachments are the anxiety produced when they are in danger and the pain produced when they break. There can be love without attachment, and this is the ultimate goal of the serious meditator, but do not pursue it too hastily, unless you want to become a mystic. If you enjoy your attachments when they are safe, do not fear to lose them, and grieve them adequately when they break, you are OK.

The third confusion with love is between conditional, unconditional, and absolute love. Conditional love is very common. You love someone because it gives you pleasure. You enjoy the way he or she looks, how he or she treats you, the gifts he or she gives to you, his or her amiability to you, even his or her worldly position or his or her material possessions. This is not bad; it is the normal kind of love, and everybody does it. You may run into problems if you try to fit into somebody's exigencies to get his or her love, or, the other way around, if you try to change somebody to fit him or her into your expectations. If you avoid those two common pitfalls, plain vulgar love may work for you.

When you love something as it is and you feel pleasure because the object of your love exists, regardless of any other circumstances, this is unconditional object love. It is unconditional because there are no conditions;

the object of your love has to fill no demands to deserve it. It is object love because it applies to someone or to something; there is an objective, a receptor, an object of your love. Mothers usually have a lot of unconditional love for their children, even if they have some conditional one as well.

Absolute unconditional love is so unconditional that it does not need an object. It is love without an object. In the normal situation, a person appears to the mind and arouses love. Can be your mother or your lover or someone to whom you profess this affect, or even a physical place or an abstract idea. This love is not fully unconditional, even as it may appear so, because it still needs the mental presence of this person to happen—this is why we call it unconditional object love. Absolute love is totally unconditional, does not need an object, it is a pure feeling state without other contents. Absolute love is the truly constructive feeling of love.

You may develop the feeling of *absolute love* proceeding by steps. First, meditate on the feeling you have for somebody you love, feel the love you have for this person, and accept everything *you do not love* about this person. Renounce to all conditions attached, especially to your desire that he or she loves you. Purify your love, that is, transform it into unconditional object love. Do not be perfectionistic; it is only a question of feeling love, does not matter what. When you are concentrating on unconditional object love, move your attention away from the object and be mindful of the state of love. Maintain this love experience alive in all your being, without paying much attention to body feelings, thoughts, images, and the like that may arise. You know the technique; it is simple passive concentration on the feeling of unconditional love.

A particular situation arises when you love someone who is suffering. To be unconditional about your love, you would have to be pleased by this person as he or she is, including his or her suffering. Yet, this would conflict with the basic intention gearing all your mindfulness training, which is the removal of suffering. The love for a person who suffers evolves quite naturally to *compassion*, which is a complex mixing of love and the intention of removing suffering. If it were not for compassion, you would not love a suffering person, unless you think there is some worth in suffering.[93]

Suffering does not exist in itself but is only the signal that a feeling is strongly unpleasant. It is not an opinion about circumstances, as feelings are, but a measure of the degree of jam in the emotion-feeling process. Without compassion, your obvious choice is to avoid and reject suffering people, because the contagion of their strongly unpleasant emotions would make you uncomfortable. You may even get angry at them, especially if the blocked emotion that is making them suffer is anger.

The obvious definition that compassion is the mixing of love with the intention of removing suffering is misleading. You may remove the suffering of a drug addict by peddling drugs to him, but this is not compassion. If you teach a drug addict to be happy without intoxicating himself, this is compassion, even if he has to suffer in the process. The concept of "removing suffering" has to be qualified by "how" you do remove it. In fact, if you remember your training with feeling meditation, you had to accept some suffering to let your feelings flow. The usual untrained way to avoid suffering is by trying to block the emotion-feeling process, which only brings more suffering and makes the matter worse. When you get the live-experience of compassion, you would realize that it boils down to helping the suffering person to create a world where suffering does not exist, more or less the same thing you are doing for yourself with this course.

The Transmutation of Feelings

Transmutation means changing something of little value into something of high value, like plumb in gold. By comparison, we talk about transmuting feelings when we transform a disturbing feeling into a constructive one. It is the ultimate achievement of feeling meditation, and it is to be attempted only after some practice with meditation on feelings.

After mastering love meditation, you may try your first approach to the transmutation of hate into love. Loving your enemies, as Jesus advised, is the ultimate act of love. However, I think that "love thy enemies" is impossible. Jesus said it in old Hebrew and in complicated circumstances, and something got lost in translation. If you love someone, he or she is not your enemy, and if he or she is your enemy, you may feel for him or her anything but love. Yet I am not here to do biblical hermeneutics but to teach about mental dynamics. Jesus was a great master, and he said something very important about the transmutation of feelings.

Concepts and live-experiences have more or less well-delineated borders, which sometimes overlap while at other times separates them distinctly. To feel love and, at the same time, be aware of the existence of somebody who minds you harm are quite distant live-experiences. To combine them is a feat as that performed by the Chinese when they combine "opportunity" and "danger" to get the concept of "crisis."[94] Only, in this case, we are not combining concepts, but two feeling states, absolute love and the live-experience of an enemy.

To feel at ease with your worst enemy, you have to go through feeling meditation on destruction, jealousy, betrayal, and the like. This procedure is close to the Tibetan practice of *Ton Glen*, which is a little bit dangerous. It consists on meditating on evil without aversion nor desire, a too far advanced practice for anybody who does not want to become a full-time mystic.[95] Transmutation is a far easier and practical approach.

To transmute your feelings, first, get in the meditation state and concentrate on the feeling of absolute love. Then, add a mental image of the person who is causing you harm or suffering. Do not force any particular aspect. She or he may come in all her or his wrath and ugly hate or may appear smiling and friendly; the image may be vivid as a video-clip or fuzzy and blurry. That is fine. You maintain now a split concentration in the feeling state of unconditional love and in the mental image of your foe. Apply passive acceptance to everything else. Accept fear, rage, sadness, or anything else that may appear with passive acceptance, that is, without clinging nor rejection. You already master passive acceptance; it is the key to the whole method. Keep your mind in unconditional love and in your foe. It does not mean that you love your foe—this would be *object love*. You just keep yourself in the state of absolute love, and at the same time, you are mindful of your foe's image.

If the negative feelings that arise are so powerful that your passive acceptance does stagger, accept that your passive acceptance does stagger, and keep at it. If this fails, try to change a little the image of your foe. You may get a memory of him or her in a good mood or smiling or less threatening and hateful. This is a trick. You are cheating a little bit, as this is not full passive acceptance, but it is not so bad. It is like putting little extra wheels on your bicycle when you are learning to ride. It is all right, as far as you know that the trick is a learning device that you are ready to discard as soon as you can.

When your mind stabilizes, and you are comfortable with the split concentration, you may try the opposite trick: enhance the viciousness of your foe's image, his frightening and hateful traits. This way you are training to maintain the fully unconditional love state in more difficult circumstances. Do not overdo the learning or training devices; they are to be discarded as soon as you can. Keep pure to the method, even if you may cheat now and then for the sake of progress.

As you proceed with the transmutation of hate, you would get more comfortable with your feelings and with your enemy, and you would see more clearly the whole situation. Remember that feelings are limbic-system opinions about the circumstances and that accepting your feelings is the same as accepting yourself. However, the circumstances themselves may be unacceptable; sometimes you have to change them. The point is that you are much more effective in changing the external world if you do not waste your energies arguing with yourself. Accepting your feelings—not blocking the emotion-feeling process—leaves you more at ease with yourself and in better condition to develop a clear idea of what is to be done and how you would do it. Unbending intent requires a lot of energy, and that is what you get when you renounce to interfere with the emotion-feeling process.

If what comes out, in the end, is that you have to fight and defend yourself, always remember the four laws of Aikido[96]:

(1) Do not cause harm.

(2) Do not allow harm to happen to you.

(3) Do not allow harm to happen to others.

(4) If you have to break rule 1 to make rules 2 or 3, do the least possible harm.

Often, you discover that your enemy wants harm to you because he or she is suffering. Some unbearable feelings, such as anger, jealousy, envy, or perhaps fear, are overflowing his processing abilities and his taking it at you is an ignorant strategy to deal with those unbearable feelings. The awareness of his suffering, incredible as it sounds, may steer you to feel compassion for your hateful enemy. Perhaps this is what Jesus meant.

Of course, you should not allow your enemy to harm you, not only because this is no good for you, but also because harming you will increase his or her unhappiness in the long run. The Aikido laws will guide you to fight with compassion.

You can apply transmutation to other burdensome feelings. It is a magnificent tool for the handling of mourning and the healing of broken bonds in general. Some so-called "Treatment-resistant depressions" are, in reality, the clinical expression of pathological grief. They may not respond well to antidepressant medications or cognitive-behavioral-therapy, but they do well to the advanced autogenic method I have called *decathexis,* which is a sophisticated clinical application of the transmutation of feelings.

Decathexis, along with other important methods, such as autogenic modification, autogenic analysis, and autogenic reconstruction which will be approached in the next coming book 2, *Clinical Autogenics,*

10.

THE INTERNAL WORLD

This chapter will introduce you to advanced experience in dynamic meditation and set the ground for inner transformation. Before you try, make sure that you are proficient in somatosensory meditation and feeling meditation. You may write to me or join one of my seminars if you feel the need for more information.

To start, first, remember one of the moments during somatosensory meditation when you were totally absorbed by the experience. Second, remember other times when you were dimly aware of the activity lurking in the back of your mind. Now, third, remember when the activity in your inner world lured you away from your concentration, and you caught yourself getting distracted. Of course, in compliance with my technical instructions, you did abandon the distractions and returned to the double concentration in the autogenic formula and the somatic experience.

If you review now the ranking of right concentration (How to Handle Distractions? pp. 85–86), you can classify the different moments of your somatosensory meditative experience in one of the following six levels:

1. Total absorption on the experience.
2. Dim awareness of something coming to your mind, but you keep in focus.
3. Your attention begins to divide itself between the focus and something else; you realize it and center yourself right away into the focus.
4. Your attention gets hooked into something, and you lose the focus momentarily; you realize it right away, leave the distraction, and come back to the focus.
5. You begin to get lost into daydreaming or falling asleep; you realize it, you renounce to the distraction, and you come back to the focus.
6. You get lost in daydreaming of fall asleep. You better finish the exercise, read chapter 6 once more, and try again from the beginning.

If you are oscillating between levels one and two most of the time, you are optimally practicing basic autogenics. The other levels are opportunities to train your attention to go back to levels one and two.

Passive concentration is fixing your attention on the autogenic focus, without any expectation or demand. Passive acceptance is, in a way, the opposite of passive concentration. Images, memories, and other contents may come to your awareness, but you ignore them, you *pass* so much that you do not even care to reject them. At the same time, you accept that those elements come to your mind, but do not entertain them. In level one of right concentration, there is total passive concentration. In level two, there is passive concentration *and* passive acceptance. As you escalate the other levels, passive concentration and passive acceptance decrease, and distractions (wandering or disperse attention) increase.

It does not matter how well trained in basic somatosensory meditation you are; there is always a tendency to drift away toward level three and beyond. But it does not matter, as soon as you notice that you are drifting into level three, return to passive concentration in mental contact and the autogenic formula. In nautical terms, passive concentration is the anchor that moors you into the somatosensory experience, while passive acceptance keeps you aware of the currents and winds.

If you wish, you may now give a try to the method invented by Luthe, "autogenic abreaction." The intent of this invention was, more than exploring the internal world, to facilitate its optimal organization, neutralizing (i.e., eliminating the disturbing potential of) traumatic and contradictory engrams. More geared towards inner exploration is the "Advanced Analytic Autogenic Training" developed by Wallnöfer, which has been recognized as a significant contribution both to psychoanalysis and to autogenics.

Continuing with the seaman's metaphor, we may say that autogenic abreaction is like sailing freely into the sea of your mind. To do it, just take the anchor of concentration aweigh and open to the experience. Stop repeating the autogenic formula, liberate your body from mental contact, keep passive acceptance all the time, and let the flow of consciousness evolve by itself. Do not indulge in any particular thought, nor allow *rèveries* to unfold. You may get into peaceful, quiet darkness, or you may see vivid colors, get flashes from your childhood, thoughts about your daily chores, or remember something you have to do. It does not matter; I am naming a few possibilities only to give you the idea that anything is possible. For the time being, do it just for a short period. Take it as only a test, a sample, a demo, for the moment. Add this short exercise at the end of your daily somatosensory meditation; it consists of only a few minutes of "doing nothing," of pure passive acceptance. Whatever happens is what was meant to happen. After you terminate the exercise, take a short note of the experience in your meditation notebook.

The Origins of the Internal World

The short exercise of "doing nothing" gave you a glimpse of your inner world. The external world is familiar to all; you perceive everything around you through your senses, and most people present tend to agree about it with you. But the internal world is highly personal and non-transferable. Each of us creates his or her own internal world through consciousness. You may say that, when you are very intimate with someone, you both share parts of your inner worlds. In fact, this is a good definition of intimacy: the sharing of inner worlds. Some gifted seers and experienced meditators may have occasional glimpses of other people's internal worlds. But those are exceptions to the basic rule: you create your internal world, and you are its sole inhabitant. The internal world is not a copy of the external world, but a highly personal construction, modeled by your personality, your previous experiences, even by your mood of the moment.

The internal world has no physical reality; it is not a place but a process, a process that requires the physical reality of your brain to produce the virtual reality of your mind.[97] The first step of the process is registering or incorporating the perceptions; this is not a simple storage of independent elements, but a fitting integration into ever-changing constructs. Each new perception modulates, modifies, and gives new meaning to previous information.

To further complicate matters, the human brain also creates its own information, reinterpreting, recombining, developing, and extrapolating what is already in the internal world. At times, the fitting of new perceptions and concepts is so difficult that some get rejected or modified. A certain rigidity of constructs is necessary; otherwise, the processing capacity of the brain would be overwhelmed by information overload, such is the multiplicity and the variety of stimuli that continuously reach our senses. But balance is necessary because excessive rigidity would prevent learning and personal growth.

The intention behind attention also counts because it filters perceptions, allowing entry only to those related to the task at hand. During active concentration, selective attention may increase repetitive performance, while decreasing the ability to create or find alternatives and new solutions. The flexibility of constructs to incorporate new information is a measure of creativity, defined as *the ability to form new connections between previously independent constructs.*[98] Passive concentration, not being concerned with goal attainment, frees attention to be fully receptive, with no more limits than those imposed by the brain's processing ability.

Depending on the ease of access to consciousness, the internal world may be divided in at least three strata:

(1) The superficial stratum, on a direct relationship with your current experience of the external world. As you are reading this, all the information you are learning is being stored and integrated with everything you knew about the subject, together with other details of your environment, the people you are with, even your current mood and behavior. This is the normal experience of life, with a continuous interplay between the external and the internal worlds. Most people find difficult to keep a clear boundary between both worlds and may get lost in their thoughts—internal world—instead of paying attention to what is going on, and vice versa.

(2) The deep stratum, initially created in the interplay with the external world, like stratum one, but following its own dynamics afterward and being continuously deformed, disintegrated, recreated, reintegrated, extrapolated, and reconstructed. This is the stratum of creativity, fantasy, and dreams. Pierre Janet called it "the subconscious," and Freud further differentiated it in "the preconscious" and "the unconscious." Both doctors were right in many things, but both missed the point that the perception of the inner world is a matter of amplitude of consciousness.

(3) The archaic stratum, even deeper than stratum two, formed before any significant relation with the external world, created by the own inner workings of the organism, common to all humans and probably to all living beings. It is the seat of human nature, universal dynamics, and, according to Carl Jung, of the archetypes and other inborn knowledge.

What Is Consciousness?

Consciousness is often defined as the awareness of oneself and the environment, but I find more operative to say that consciousness is an active process that integrates, stores, and modifies the perceptions of oneself and of the own circumstances. Of course, you are always aware—at some level—of your perceptions, so consciousness entails awareness. Being conscious of the own consciousness— "being aware of being aware"—is considered an extraordinary human achievement, known as self-awareness, not to be confused with self-consciousness.[99] The brain is the chief organizer and the main physical seat of the internal world, but consciousness is larger than the brain; it impregnates every cell of your body. It may even exist beyond your body. Nevertheless, in the usual human circumstances, consciousness is maintained by active and permanent brain processes. There are two general aspects of consciousness to consider: the level and the state.

The level of consciousness. Consciousness is an active process that requires effort and energy. The level of consciousness is related to alertness and wakefulness; it depends on the energy available for the processes of attention, perception, integration, and storage of information. The clarity and cohesion of mental contents are regulated by the level of consciousness.

The neurological structure more directly in charge of the level of consciousness is the reticular activating system, also known as the ascending reticular formation or simply reticular formation (see pp. 56 and 61 and endnote 56). The levels of consciousness are routinely explored by neurologists and anesthetists, who usually distinguish a variable number of gradual levels, ranging from normal wakefulness to the vegetative state (i.e., awake, confused, drowsy, stuporous, comatose, vegetative).

The state of consciousness. You are not aware of all your inner world at a given moment, only of a part of it. A person with unified consciousness would be aware of everything in her range of perception and, at the same time, of the total activity of her mind and its mental contents. However, the fragmentation of consciousness in many different states is the rule of the human condition. Buddha regarded this condition as a consequence of the impermanence of the ego, and Gurdjieff described it as the coexistence of many egos that compete with each other for the control of your life. The common goal of all human-development schools is the unification of consciousness, a process that is known by different names, such as amplification of consciousness, remembering oneself, transcending the ego, liberating oneself from automatisms, self-awareness, illumination, and the like.

The state of consciousness is related to the temporary contents of consciousness, including not only data and mental representations, but also transformational processes, programs of behavior, points of view, attitudes, and patterns of action. In my definition, *a state of consciousness is the set of mental constructs operative at a given moment.*

You may change from one state to another maintaining the illusion of your "I" as unique, even as your behavior may change quite a bit from state to state. An experienced observer may identify the changes of your state of consciousness by recurrent patterns of subjectiveness (how do you think and feel) and of behavior (what you do).

Some state or states usually predominate, while others appear rarely or only under exceptional circumstances. The predominant constructs of a state regulate your perception of the external world. Those precepts which are concordant with the construct are incorporated without resistance, further reinforcing the construct. On the contrary, the perceptions that do not fit the construct are rejected. The predominant state of consciousness controls your perception and your behavior in the external world, not always with your full awareness and permission.

Even memories can vary from state to state, a phenomenon known as "state-dependent learning." You may know something in a given state, forget it completely when you change to another state, and remember it clearly when you return to the first state. There are many everyday examples, as when you wake up from a dream with a very clear recollection of it, only to discover at breakfast that you only remember vague details. Or you may decide that you need something from another room, forget what it was when you get there, and quickly remember it when you go back to the room where you took the decision.

The neurological structures directly regulating the states of consciousness are the two brain hemispheres, or, more exactly, the interplay between them and the relative dominance of each one (see pp. 66–72).

The fluency of consciousness is the degree of ease to change its level or state. A state of consciousness is fluid when has flexible boundaries and connects easily with other states. The amplitude of consciousness is the amount of constructs and modes of conceptualization it may contain. Training in autogenics increases the fluency and the amplitude of consciousness. This would allow you to remember yourself better from state to state, and to discover contradictions and inconsistencies in your inner world. With the widening of consciousness, your maladaptive automatisms tend to disappear, you manage better your circumstances, and your behavior becomes more appropriate to your life-plan.

The Cartography of the Internal World

Cartography is the science of maps. A map helps you to know where you are and where you are going. In the last century, there was an increased interest in mapping the internal world, to provide visual analogs of mental processes.[100]

Words are quite inefficient to describe psychological states, so seers have turned since remote antiquity to images, paintings, and metaphors.[101] Maps of consciousness are a metaphor, drawings that seek to add a sense of continuity and globalness to the limitation of words. Tart, one of the pioneers in the scientific study of consciousness, has provided interesting graphic descriptions of his theory on state formation and dissolution. Horowitz has applied the cartography of *states of mind* to psychotherapy and created a method he called *configurational analysis*. Eric Berne very aptly explains his transactional analysis with helpful diagrams of all the possible *ego states*, showing how they relate to each other at the intrapersonal and interpersonal levels.

MAP OF AMPLIFIED STATES OF CONSCIOUSNESS

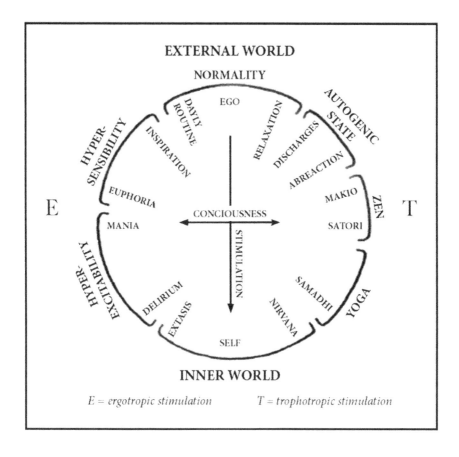

EXTERNAL WORLD

NORMALITY

EGO

HYPER-SENSIBILITY

DAYLY ROUTINE

INSPIRATION

RELAXATION

AUTOGENIC STATE

DISCHARGES

ABREACTION

EUPHORIA

MAKIO

ZEN

E

CONCIOUSNESS

T

MANIA

SATORI

HYPER-EXCITABILITY

STIMULATION

DELIRIUM

EXTASIS

NIRVANA

SAMADHI

YOGA

SELF

INNER WORLD

E = ergotropic stimulation   T = trophotropic stimulation

Above all of them, Roland Fisher has elaborated a complete "Cartography of the Ecstatic and Meditative States," based on electrophysiological measures and psychological descriptions. Fisher's great contribution was the discovery that both ergotropic and trophotropic stimulation detach the attention from the external world and amplify the field of inner consciousness. He mapped the ergotropic path by taking his information from psychedelic and psychiatric studies, and the trophotropic side from meditative experiences.

At variance with the other authors, Fisher was not concerned with the relations among different partial states but with the global aspect of consciousness. From the concrete ego of normality, there is a progressive widening of consciousness, maximum in the manic state on the ergotropic side and in the satori state on the trophotropic side, and from there a progressive narrowing, maximum in the total self-absorption of the ecstatic and nirvana states. Following his approach, I have included the autogenic state in the Map of Amplified States of Consciousness.

The vertical arrow on the map indicates the progression of inner consciousness, from everyday contact with the external world to complete absorption on the self in the nirvana state. The full process, which is long, difficult and of questionable practical interest, is the aim of the mystic schools that follow the Vedanta precept (Bhagavad Gita, 2:71-72):

They are forever free who renounce all selfish desires and break away from the ego-cage of "I," "me" and "mine" to be united with the Lord. This is the supreme state. Attain to this, and pass from death to immortality.

The horizontal arrow indicates the amplitude of consciousness. There is a progressive widening from the normal state to the Zen state, and then a gradual narrowing to end in total self-absorption in the nirvana state.

In the ergotropic side, the consciousness widens to a maximum in the manic psychiatric disorders and then narrows to the extreme in mystical ecstasy. The trophotropic path requires a long effort in mind-brain training, which gives the meditator a great control of the experience and an increasing ability to integrate the disparate contents of his internal world. By contrast, those under the influence of drugs or psychiatric disorders in the trophotropic path are often overwhelmed by their "inner trip" and unable to make any sense of their experience.

In the state of *normality*, consciousness is in contact with both the external and the internal worlds, attention can easily move outward and inward, and there is a continuous interchange between both worlds. As the trophotropic stimulation progress, the proportion internal world or external world increases, and the cognitive contents of the state of consciousness come even less from the superficial stratum and even more from the deep and archaic strata.

The *autogenic state* is the meditative state closest to normality. Our studies on the subjective experience of the autogenic state with the application of the Questionnaire of States of Consciousness (see appendix) have been able to differentiate three key features of the autogenic state:
(1) The underlying feeling of tranquility and peacefulness, which correspond to the direct limbic response to mild trophotropic activation.
(2) The increased perception of inner experience, both physical and psychological, which corresponds to the widening of consciousness in the superficial stratum.
(3) The autogenic discharges, sudden phenomena of sensorial, motor, visceral, visual, or emotional nature, which correspond to brief incursions of elements from the deep and archaic strata.

In the *Zen state*, consciousness is at its widest, achieving the whole perception of inner and outer reality in *satori*. Even if the Zen meditator seems totally immersed in his or her inner world, his or her perception of the external world is maintained or even enhanced. A version of Zen meditation is meditation in action, full concentration in what one is doing, essential in martial arts and in various Japanese ceremonies. The *makyo* are hallucinatory phenomena that may appear in this state, similar to the visual discharges of the autogenic state, but more intense and convincing. The Zen monks describe the makyo either as terrifying demons or as beautiful girls, both with the common purpose of stranding the monk away from his mystical pursuit.

In the *Yoga state*, there is a progressive narrowing of the consciousness of both the internal and the external worlds, which ends in the total absorption of the self on nirvana. The progress from the normal state to samadhi, full concentrative absorption, and to nirvana, complete self-unification, can be made by a strict following of the *samatha* method or by the more familiar combination of *vipassana* and *samatha*. In any case, passage through all previous states, an experience that is not always pleasant, is not easy to avoid.

Hemispheric Cooperation

Luthe attributed the widening of consciousness during the autogenic state to the increased activity of the right hemisphere (The Second Autogenic Switch, see p. 70) and the autogenic discharges to the enhancement of interhemispheric communication. The results of our TABS study seem to confirm both hypotheses. Return to page 70 and have a look at the fMRI images showing increased right-brain activity during the autogenic state. You may also review the discussion of the specialized cognitive functions of the two brain hemispheres.

The increased activation of right-brain cognitive processes is the neurological substratum of the amplified states of consciousness. As the widening of consciousness proceeds, the awareness of the internal world increases. First, there is amplified access in the autogenic state to the superficial stratum, whose contents are easily amenable to words. Interhemispheric cooperation is not usually problematic at this point because most right-brain representations have verbal equivalents in the left brain.

At further amplification of the state, elements from the other strata become increasingly accessible. Most of the deep stratum and all of the archaic stratum (you may review pp. 150–152) are experiential and do not have preregistered verbal equivalents. Interhemispheric cooperation begins to get difficult at this point. The often-reported ineffable nature of the mystic and meditative experiences have its basis on this difficulty. The usual *vipassana* and especially the *samatha* meditations allow the increased activity of the right brain to proceed, renouncing to the cooperation of the left brain. The autogenics approach follows a different path. Training interhemispheric cooperation is one of the fundamental goals of autogenics, manifest since the very beginning of your training. Dual concentration, the unique brand of autogenic somatosensory meditation, coordinates the somatic live-experience (right brain) with its verbal formulation (left brain). This explains the enhanced interhemispheric communication demonstrated by our TABS Study (see fMRI images in the next pages)

Training of interhemispheric cooperation continues in advanced autogenics. Appropriate training in autogenic somatosensory meditation is necessary, not only to favor the learning and development of *passive acceptance,* but also because interhemispheric cooperation becomes more challenging and precise in the advanced methods.

ENHANCED INTERHEMISPHERIC COMMUNICATION 1

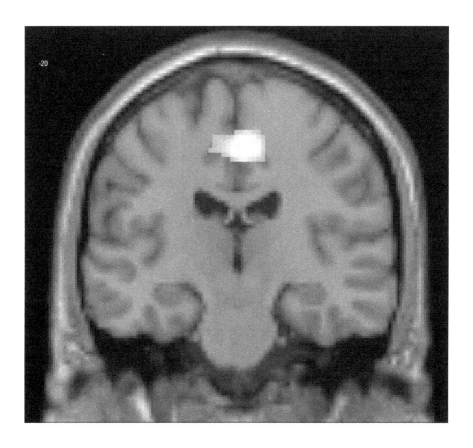

fMRI coronal view of the brain during the autogenic state, showing bilateral activation on both sides of the frontal lobe.

For better images of the TABS study, you may enter
www.icat.world

ENHANCED INTERHEMISPHERIC COMMUNICATION- 2

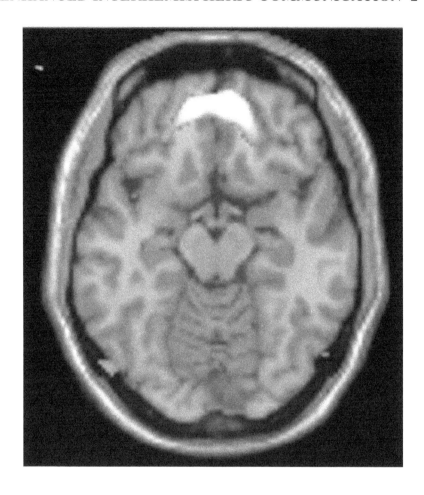

fMRI transversal view of the brain during the autogenic state, showing bilateral activation on both sides of the frontal lobe.

To see more of the TABS study, you may enter

www.icat.world

Feeling meditation would be entirely experiential were it not for the minimum left-brain participation on the naming of feelings. More demanding is translating the increasing nonverbal live-experiences into words, the essential part of the method of autogenic abreaction. Autogenic abreaction and autogenic analysis, together with autogenic modification, will be further discussed in book 2, *Clinical Autogenics*.

The interhemispheric cooperation, activated in the autogenic state, is essential for creativity and mental health. As your state of consciousness enlarges, you become aware of nonverbal experiences stored in your right brain, and interhemispheric communication helps you to find a left-brain equivalent. The exact word may come easily, or you may have to resort to poetry, painting, music, or some other symbolic representation. Some right-brain experiences have never been verbal. The archaic stratum, for instance, was formed before you had access to words. Parts of the deep stratum are preverbal, and some of those which are post verbal may lack appropriate words, either because of their ineffable nature or because there was a break in interhemispheric communication at the time of their formation.

The unique autogenic dual concentration provides simultaneous concordant information to both hemispheres, enhancing interhemispheric cooperation and hence interhemispheric communication. Concordant information means that the verbal and the nonverbal components of the information are consistent and equivalent. If I say, "This ball is round," this is concordant information. It may sound

INTERHEMISPHERIC COHERENCE BY CONCORDANCE

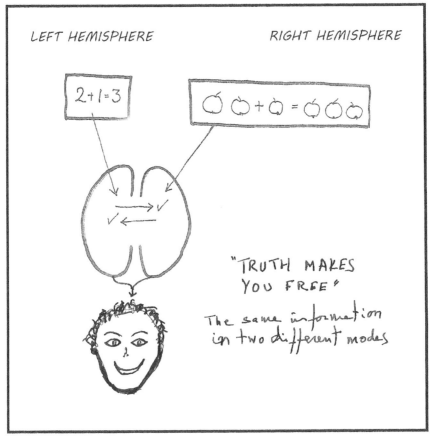

Modified from Luthe, Lettres sur l'Education, 1975

banal, but it is concordant. If I show you three apples and I say, "1 apple + 1 apple + 1 apple = 3 apples," I am teaching you to add, but above all, I am giving you concordant information.

Because of the inquisitiveness of the human mind and our natural thirst for truth, we like concordant information. Each hemisphere stores information in its specific cognitive mode, and if those modes are concordant, there is interhemispheric coherence.

Checking back and forth concordant information gives a feeling of understanding. That is why you like to know the name of things. This is also the reason why some words appear to have no meaning; they are "empty words." They may have space in your left brain, but there is no corresponding representation in the right brain. This neurobiological discussion is relevant for chapter 3, Words, Concepts, and Life, which you may like to reread now.

The Functional Disconnection Syndrome

In 1969, the neurosurgeon Joseph Bogen and the psychologists Roger Sperry and Michel Gazzaniga described the "hemisphere disconnection syndrome" in patients who had surgical *commissurotomy*—severing of the fibers of the *corpus callosum*—to relieve their epilepsy. The communication between the two brain hemispheres was physically interrupted, and each hemisphere had then to process information on its own, without the cooperation of the other. Surprisingly, the patients led apparently normal lives, with no particular complaints related to the intervention. There were subtle deficits, however, that Sperry and Gazzaniga were able to identify with inventive research methods. But the most important part was that each hemisphere could be studied free from the influence of the other, and thus came the discovery that each side of the brain specializes in different cognitive functions. You may review the details of those findings in pages 64 to 68.

In 1975, applying the new knowledge on hemisphere specialization, Wolfgang Luthe described the "functional hemispheric disconnection syndrome," in which the interhemispheric communication was impaired, not because of physical causes, but because of alterations in information processing. Whereas, as we have seen, the concordance between verbal and experiential information facilitates the unified communication between the hemispheres, discordant information has the opposite effect. Instead of a smooth communication, there is a back and forth checking and rechecking, which produces feelings of discomfort, absurdity, and incomprehension, with increasing incoherence between the hemispheres and final breach of communication. There are two mechanisms producing functional interhemispheric disconnection: by conflict and by contradiction.

INTERHEMISPHERIC INCOHERENCE BY CONFLICT

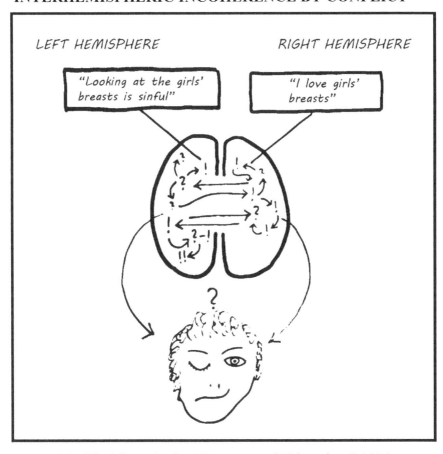

Modified from Luthe, "Lettres sur l'Education," 1975

In conflict, the information processed in one mode has a positive meaning, whereas the opposite occurs with the information processed in the other mode. Both modes are processing the same information, only with opposing emotional values. The example in the figure, made in the seventies when Quebec was staunchly Catholic, shows a child checking the pleasurable experiential information his right brain is processing, with the negative verbal information fed to his left brain. Both modes of information are compatible, only they have different effects on the happiness of the child.

The better the interhemispheric communication, the worst the discomfort produced by the conflict. Functional blocking allows ignoring the conflict and splits consciousness into two separated states, one dominated by the left brain, full of guilt and sexual inhibition, and another licentious and flirty, governed by the right brain. If this child were to go into autogenic therapy as an adult, he might get autogenic discharges related to the strict dictums of his rigid education. As treatment proceeds, the neutralization process would reduce the discomfort, whereas the increased interhemispheric cooperation would merge the conflicting states in a new amplified state in which the information becomes concordant.

The second cause of interhemispheric incoherence is contradiction, which I have dubbed *aporia,* a term I took from Greek philosophy. Aporia refers to two statements that cannot be true together, although each one of them can be true if taken separately. The psychopathological effects of aporia may be worse than those of conflict because aporia needs a stronger blocking to prevent experiencing the incoherence. Gregory Bateson, from his studies in family dynamics, formulated the *double bind hypothesis of schizophrenia*, which sustains that if contradictory information—aporia—is continuously given to a child, he or she may develop a severe psychiatric illness. *Triple bind* would be a better name for Bateson's theory because a third element has to be added to the two incompatible informations: the permanent prohibition to recognize and expose the contradiction.

INTERHEMISPHERIC INCOHERENCE BY APORIA

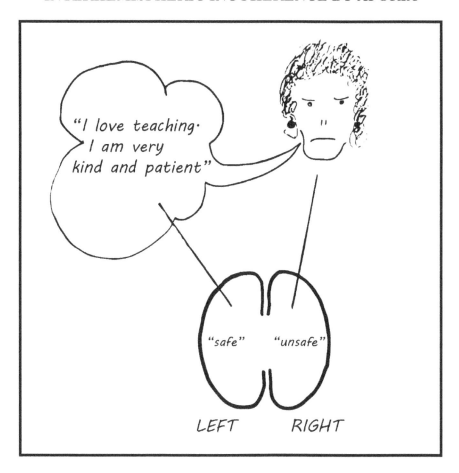

Modified from Luthe, "Lettres sur l'Education," 1975

Notice in the previous figure the facial expression of disgust and anger of a teacher, and compare it with the kind words she is saying. This is *aporia* because both pieces of information cannot be true at the same time. The recipient may combine both statements in one that is concordant, such as "this dangerous bitch is lying" and thus preserve hemispheric coherence. A more flexible and creative formulation could be "This lady may be nice, but she seems prone to bad moods; let's watch her." Both solutions prevent interhemispheric blocking; both dissolve the *aporia*. The first one is rigid but definitive; the second one is more open but more effort demanding. The first offers security at the expense of empathy; the second opens the way to interpersonal understanding, at the cost of certitude.

Creativity and States of Consciousness

Creativity is the ability to express something that, at least in part, originates inside oneself. The most intense productivity is not creative if merely reproduces elements from the external world. The most intense inner life is not creative if its workings are not embodied in the world of external reality.

The two personal marks of creativity are originality and manifestation. Creativity is not only at the basis of art, science, design, and problem solving but also of human development. In this case, the manifestation of the new person is in his or her life change, his or her authenticity,[102] his or her new ways of interaction, his or her capacity of response and influence.

There is a third mark of creativity, called the proof of reality, which basically boils down to the evidence that the creation is better than what already exists. This mark is not strictly personal and may be hindered by external dynamics alien to creativity, such as envy or resistance to change. Some creative persons come "before their age," what means that their creations take a long time to be validated.

The first personal mark, originality, requires a reorganization of the internal world. The different perceptions of a given aspect of the external world accumulate and configure a construct or cognitive scheme that represents this external reality at the neuronal level. In the beginning, the construct is susceptible of continuous modification, but, as it incorporates increasing amounts of data, it becomes rigid and would require a highly discordant information to change. New data that confirms what is already in the construct will be labeled as redundant and not be given much attention. Discrepant data that does not fit in a rigidified construct will receive even less attention and be rejected. Concordant perceptions strengthen and solidify the construct. Discordant perceptions are either distorted to fit in the construct or outright ignored. This is why people who know can't learn.

At some point, the accumulation of discrepant data becomes outrageous enough to force the revision and modification of the construct. This comes readily to those who are not attached to their knowledge. Believers have it hard, as they invest a lot of self-importance on knowing the truth. Creative scientists have it easier, as they feel comfortable with uncertainty and think that conviction is only lack of data. This is the first step of the *creative act: a remodeling of the interior reality, a new way of seeing things, a change, sometimes abrupt, of our conceptual schemes.* The creation of a new reality begins in the mind.

The second personal mark of creativity is manifestation, the production in the external world of an equivalent of what is being formed in the inner world. This second step is driven by the pressure to maintain the concordance between the inner world and the outer worlds. It is the same force that opposes the perception of all reality that does not conform with the inner world, only it operates in the opposite direction. Instead of encapsulating rigid constructs, this force opens them and seeks their actualization in the external world.

I have named this force *Creative Tension* and defined it as *"the pressure exerted by the new constructs formed in the inner world to have their equivalents in the outer world."*[103]

An idea is operative from the moment it is born. The subjective perception of the creative tension changes as the creative process unfolds, following a series of overlapping steps.

The cognitive steps of creativity

1. Discovery of common patterns in different events. Some connections are perceived between previously separated perceptions or constructs. Creative tension begins.
2. Formation of new constructs in which previously unconnected patterns have evident correspondence and interaction. The diffuse connections perceived in phase one reorganize to form a stable structure.
3. Reorganization of the internal world to accommodate the new constructs. A new inner reality appears. The world is seen in a new way.
4. Externalization of this new reality. Intense interhemispheric cooperation to formulate the new inner reality in words and plans. The external world has to change to accommodate the new inner reality.

The feeling steps of creativity

1. Curiosity and wondering. Awakening of creative tension as inquisitiveness and want for novelty.
2. Enthusiasm at the discovery of something new. The penny drops. Suddenly everything clicks. The *Eureka* experience.
3. Effort, desire, and frustration. Creative tension is at its peak. The pressure may be uncomfortable.
4. Struggle, conviction, longing for recognition and acceptance.

To Be Continued – in the next book.

The only way to change the future is to change the past.

There are two pasts:

The external past, the one lived by everybody who was around then and there. This does not exist anymore, so there is nothing to change.

The internal past, the one engraved in the transformations your body has been making since you lived then and there. This past exists and is in continuous operation. This is the one past you can change, and you better do it, if you want your future to be different.

This book comes to its end. You know now a lot about attention, feelings, inner experience and self-development. There is still much left. There is much to learn about autogenic modification, autogenic analysis, and autogenic reconstruction.

Transmutation of feelings, for instance, is a magnificent tool for the healing of broken bonds, for the handling of mourning, and for the treatment of pathological grief. This is the method called *decathexis*. All that, and other themes, with clinical examples, are left now for the coming autogenics book 2, *Clinical Autogenics*.

APPENDIX

QUESTIONNAIRE OF STATES OF CONSCIOUSNESS

The Subjective Experience of Meditation

QUESTIONNAIRE OF STATES OF CONSCIOUSNESS
The Subjective Experience of Meditation

(C) Luis de Rivera, 1990
ICAT Information Center
Avenida de Filipinas, 52 – 8 b
28003 Madrid. Spain

Name:…………………………………………………………….

Sex.:…………...Civil Status: ……...Date of Birth:…………..

Profession:……… .... Date of Today .... …

Name of your meditation method…………………………………

For how long you meditate? Years │ __ │ months │ __ │ weeks │ __ │

How often do you meditate…Daily. How many times? │ __ │

Weekly. How many times? │ __ │

Average duration in minutes of each meditation exercise │ _ _ │

Your practice of meditation is:

Regular │ __ │ Sporadic │ __ │ Only when I need it. │ __ │

Your exercises of meditation induce a certain state of consciousness. Please, check in the following list the number corresponding to the intensity or frequency of the subjective phenomena you may experience.

If it does not happen at all, check │ 0 │
If it is present with low intensity or very seldom, check │ 1 │
If it is present with moderate intensity or frequency, check │ 2 │
If it is present with high intensity or frequency, check │ 3 │
If it is present with very high intensity or almost always, check │ 4 │

179

1. It is clearly different from the usual state of awareness
| 0 | | 1 | | 2 | | 3 | | 4 |

2. I only experience this state practicing the exercise
| 0 | | 1 | | 2 | | 3 | | 4 |

3. Before my training in meditation I had
spontaneously experienced similar states
| 0 | | 1 | | 2 | | 3 | | 4 |

4. The experience of this state is pleasant.
| 0 | | 1 | | 2 | | 3 | | 4 |
.
5. The experience of this state is unpleasant
| 0 | | 1 | | 2 | | 3 | | 4 |

6. I experience clear sensations of relaxation and inner peace
| 0 | | 1 | | 2 | | 3 | | 4 |

7. I experience clear sensations of safety
| 0 | | 1 | | 2 | | 3 | | 4 |

8. I experience clear sensations of unconcern.
| 0 | | 1 | | 2 | | 3 | | 4 |

9. I experience clear sensations of self-confidence
| 0 | | 1 | | 2 | | 3 | | 4 |

10. I experience clear sensations of feeling
that everything will turn out fine.
| 0 | | 1 | | 2 | | 3 | | 4 |

11. I feel that I exist beyond my own individuality
| 0 | | 1 | | 2 | | 3 | | 4 |

12. I feel merged with a universal entity (God, cosmos, etc.).
| 0 | | 1 | | 2 | | 3 | | 4 |

13. I feel as if my usual fears and worries have no reason to be
| 0 | | 1 | | 2 | | 3 | | 4 |

14. I experience sensations of drowsiness
| 0 | | 1 | | 2 | | 3 | | 4 |

15. I experience sensations of inner freedom, of not being restrained by usual constraints and pressures
| 0 | | 1 | | 2 | | 3 | | 4 |

16. I feel the sensation of inner strength, an increase in my energy and capacity
| 0 | | 1 | | 2 | | 3 | | 4 |

17. I am more aware of sensations, emotions, and worries
| 0 | | 1 | | 2 | | 3 | | 4 |

18. Unpleasant ideas or feelings
| 0 | | 1 | | 2 | | 3 | | 4 |

19. I am aware of my feelings about other people, certain events, memories, etc
| 0 | | 1 | | 2 | | 3 | | 4 |

20. I get intuitions, bright ideas or solutions to difficult problems
| 0 | | 1 | | 2 | | 3 | | 4 |

21. I experience physical sensations of weight
| 0 | | 1 | | 2 | | 3 | | 4 |

22. I experience physical sensations of heat
| 0 | | 1 | | 2 | | 3 | | 4 |

23. I feel pulsations or hammering
| 0 | | 1 | | 2 | | 3 | | 4 |

24. I experience physical sensations of pressure.
| 0 | | 1 | | 2 | | 3 | | 4 |

25. I experience vertigo, dizziness or falling down
| 0 | | 1 | | 2 | | 3 | | 4 |

26. I experience a headache
| 0 | | 1 | | 2 | | 3 | | 4 |

27. I experience nausea, vomiting or retching
| 0 | | 1 | | 2 | | 3 | | 4 |

28. I experience sensations of floating in space
| 0 | | 1 | | 2 | | 3 | | 4 |

29. I experience physical sensations of spinning or turning
| 0 | | 1 | | 2 | | 3 | | 4 |

30. I see colors in my mind
| 0 | | 1 | | 2 | | 3 | | 4 |

31. There are flashes of brightness or luminosity
| 0 | | 1 | | 2 | | 3 | | 4 |

32. I see stripes, imprecise or abstract drawings.
| 0 | | 1 | | 2 | | 3 | | 4 |

33. I see objects, persons, situations
| 0 | | 1 | | 2 | | 3 | | 4 |

34. I see moving images or like a movie
| 0 | | 1 | | 2 | | 3 | | 4 |

35. Sensations that the body changes in size
| 0 | | 1 | | 2 | | 3 | | 4 |

36. Sensations that the body changes in shape
| 0 | | 1 | | 2 | | 3 | | 4 |

37. Sensation of being out of my body
| 0 | | 1 | | 2 | | 3 | | 4 |

38. It seems as though parts of the body were missing
| 0 | | 1 | | 2 | | 3 | | 4 |

39. Sensations of numbness
| 0 | | 1 | | 2 | | 3 | | 4 |

40. I feel cold during the exercise
| 0 | | 1 | | 2 | | 3 | | 4 |

41. I feel like cramps
| 0 | | 1 | | 2 | | 3 | | 4 |

42. Sensations of shivering
| 0 | | 1 | | 2 | | 3 | | 4 |

43. Sensation of pressure in the body
| 0 | | 1 | | 2 | | 3 | | 4 |

44. Sensations of inflammation or swelling
| 0 | | 1 | | 2 | | 3 | | 4 |

45. Sensations of pain
| 0 | | 1 | | 2 | | 3 | | 4 |

46. Strong beats or pressure over or in the heart
| 0 | | 1 | | 2 | | 3 | | 4 |

47. Breathing distracts or interferes with concentration
| 0 | | 1 | | 2 | | 3 | | 4 |

48. I feel like coughing, or I cough
| 0 | | 1 | | 2 | | 3 | | 4 |

49. I feel like sighing, or I sigh
| 0 | | 1 | | 2 | | 3 | | 4 |
.

50. Sensation of breathing better
| 0 | | 1 | | 2 | | 3 | | 4 |

51. Shortness of breath or choking
| 0 | | 1 | | 2 | | 3 | | 4 |

52. I feel emptiness in my stomach
| 0 | | 1 | | 2 | | 3 | | 4 |

53. Noises or movements in the guts
| 0 | | 1 | | 2 | | 3 | | 4 |

54. Squeezing or pressure in the stomach
| 0 | | 1 | | 2 | | 3 | | 4 |

55. Feelings of anger or rage
| 0 | | 1 | | 2 | | 3 | | 4 |

56. Sudden crying or weeping
| 0 | | 1 | | 2 | | 3 | | 4 |

57. Sudden smiling or laughing
| 0 | | 1 | | 2 | | 3 | | 4 |

58. Yawning
| 0 | | 1 | | 2 | | 3 | | 4 |

59. Sudden movements, like shaking,
trembling, startling, ticks, etc.)
| 0 | | 1 | | 2 | | 3 | | 4 |

60. Feelings of tension or anxiety
| 0 | | 1 | | 2 | | 3 | | 4 |

Add any other phenomena that are not on the list:

....

....

....

BIBLIOGRAPHY

Anonymous. *The Bhagavad Gita*. Introduced and translated by Eknath Easwaran. Nilgiri Press, Tomales, 2007

Anonymous. *La Filocalia de la Oración de Jesús* Ediciones Sígueme, Salamanca, 1985.

Anonymous. *The Way of a Pilgrim*. Shambala Publications, Boston, 1991.

Arnold, Magda B. *Emotion and Personality* Columbia University Press, New York, 1960.

Arnold, Magda B. *Feelings and Emotions* Academic Press, New York, 1970.

Baigent, Michael and Leigh, Richard. The Dead Sea Scrolls Deception. Manila: Summit Books, 1992

Baruzzo, Roberto. *Equilibrio Personale e Training Autogeno* Libreriauniversitaria.it Edizioni, Padova, 2014.

Bateson, Gregory. *Steps to an Ecology of Mind* Ballantine Books, New York, 1975

Benson, H. *The Relaxation Response*. Morrow, 1975.

Bird, Jane. *I Could Do with Some of That. The Power of Autogenics*. Sunbury, Middlesex: Legends Publishing, 2015.

Blausen.com staff. "Medical Gallery of Blausen Medical 2014." *WikiJournal of Medicine* 1, no. 2 (2014). https://doi.org/10.15347/wjm/2014.010. ISSN 2002-4436. https://commons.wikimedia.org/w/index.php?curid=3157 4257.

Brancaleone, Ferdinando. *TBA2: Metodiche Avanzate di Terapia Bionomico-Autogena.* FrancoAngelini, Milano, 2011.

Buddhaghosa, Bhadantacariya. *The Path of Purification (Visuddhimagga).* BPS Pariyatti Editions, Onalaska, 1999.

Burton, Robert E. *Self-Remembering.* Samuel Weiser, York Beach, 1995

Cabanac, Michel. *What is Emotion?* Behavioral Processes, 2002, 60:69-84

Cannon, Walter B. *Bodily Changes in Pain, Hunger, Fear and Rage.* Charles T. Branford Company, Boston, 1953.

Cannon, Walter B. *The Wisdom of the Body.* Norton. New York, 1932

Castaneda, Carlos. *The Power of Silence.* Washington Square Press, New York, 1991.

Cousins, Lance. *The Stages of Christian Mysticism and Buddhist Purification: Interior Castle of St Teresa of Ávila and the Path of Purification of Buddhaghosa.* In : K. Werner (Ed). The Yogi and the Mystic. Studies in Indian and Comparative Mysticism. Curzon Press, Richmond, Surrey, 1994, pp. 101-118

Damasio, Antonio. *The Feeling of What Happens.* Harcourt, New York, 1999

Damasio, Antonio. *Self Comes to Mind.* Pantheon, New York, 2010

De Mello, Anthony. *La Oración de la Rana.* Sal Terrae, Santander, 1988.

de Rivera, L., De Montigny, C., Remillard, G. y Andermann, F. *Autogenic Therapy of temporal lobe epilepsy*. Editor F. Antonelli. En "Therapy in Psychosomatic Medicine" Pozzi, Roma. (1977) págs. 40-47.

de Rivera, Luis. *Autogenic Abreaction and Psychoanalysis*. Editor: W. Luthe. In "Autogenic Methods: Application and Perspectives." Editorial: Pozzi, Roma. (1977) págs. l58-l63.

de Rivera Luis. *Creatividad y Estados de Conciencia*. Revista de Psicología General y Aplicada, 33: 4l5-426 (1978).

de Rivera, Luis. *Drogas, Estados de Consciencia y Creatividad.* Psiquis, 1980, 1:167-175

de Rivera, L, De Montigny, C, Remillard, G, Andermann, F. *Tratamiento psicológico de la epilepsia*. Psiquis, 2: l36-l52 (1981).

de Rivera, Luis. *Estructura y Función de la Mente Humana.* Psiquis, 1987, 8:13-20

de Rivera, Luis. *Creativity and Psychosis in Scientific Research*. American Journal of Psychoanalysis, 1993, 53:77-84

de Rivera, L y García-Trujillo, MR. *La experiencia de relajación: aplicación del cuestionario de estados de conciencia a sujetos en entrenamiento autógeno y otras formas de meditación*. Psiquis, 17:13-23 (1996).

de Rivera, Luis. *La spécialisation hémisphérique et les états de conscience*. Revue Française de Relaxation Psychothérapique, 1997, 18:81-98.

de Rivera, Luis. *Psychothérapie Autogène. En: J. Guimon and A. Fredenrich-Muhlebach: Corps et Psychotherapy.* Editions Médicine & Hygiène, Ginebra, 1997. págs. 238-248.

de Rivera, Luis. *Autogenic Psychotherapy and Psychoanalysis.* In: J. Guimon (Ed.) The body in Psychotherapy. Karger, Basilea, 1997. págs. 176-181.

de Rivera, Luis. Psicoterapia Autogena. Manual Teórico-Práctico de Iniciación Terapéutica. Klinik, Madrid, 1999

de Rivera, Luis. *Autogene Abreaktion* (pp. 56-57), *Autogene Neutralisation* (pp. 57-58), *Autogene Rekonstruction* (p. 59), *Autogene Verbalisation* (p. 59), *Entladungen, Autogene* (p. 65), In: G. Stumm y A. Pritz (Eds.) Wörterbuch der Psychotherapie. Springer Verlag. Viena, 2000

de Rivera, Luis. *Autogenic Analysis: The tool Freud was looking for.* International Journal of Psychotherapy, 2001, 6:71-76.

de Rivera, Luis: *Homeostasis, Alostasis y Adaptacion. En:* J. Guimón (Ed.), Crisis y Contencion. Eneida Madrid 2008. pp. 31-37

de Rivera, Luis. *Sindromes de Estres.* Sintesis, Madrid, 2010

de Rivera, Luis. *Crisis Emocionales.* Espasa, Madrid, 2002; Second Edition Createspace, Charleston, 2012

de Rivera, Luis. *Stati de coscienza e psicoterapia autógena.* Psyche Nuova, 2014, 33:19-32 de Rivera, Luis. *El Maltrato Psicológico*. Editorial Altaria, Tarragona, 2015.

de Rivera, Luis. *Entrenamiento Autógeno*. Klinik, 1999; Createspace, Charleston, 2015.

de Rivera, Luis. *Medicina Psicosomática*. Karpos, 1980; Createspace, Charleston, 2015.

Epictetus. *Enchiridion*. Dover Thrift Editions, New York, 2004.

Evola, Julius. *La Dottrina del Risveglio*. Edizioni Mediterranee, Roma, 1995.

Fisher, Roland. *A Cartography of the Ecstatic and Meditative States*. Science, 1971, 174:897-904

Fuster, Joaquin. *Cortex and Mind*. Oxford University Press, 2003

Gallway, W.T: *The Inner Game of Tennis*. Random House, New York, 1974

Garcia-Trujillo R, Monterrey AL y de Rivera L: *Meditación y Psicosis*. Psiquis, 13:75-79 (1992).

Gastaldo, Giovanni; Ottobre, Miranda. *Il Training Autogeno in Diretta*. Armando Editore, Roma, 2008.

Gastaldo, Giovanni; Ottobre, Miranda. *Psicoterapia Autogena in Quattro Stadi*. Armando Editore, Roma, 2008.

Gazzaniga, Michael S., and LeDoux, Joseph E. *The Integrated Mind*. Plenum Press, New York, 1978.

Gellhorn, Ernst; Loofbourrow, G. N. *Emotions & Emotional Disorders*. Harper & Row Publishers, New York, 1963.

Goleman, Daniel. *Destructive Emotions*. Bantam Book, New York, 2003.

Goleman, Daniel. *Focus*. Editorial Kairós, Barcelona, 2013.

Goleman, Daniel. *The Varieties of Meditative Experience*. Editorial Kairós, Barcelona, 1986.

Grimaldi, Carmine. *L'Attivazione del Corpo nella Psicoterapia Binomica/Autogena*. Edizioni Centro Studi Erickson, Trento, 2013.

Gunaratana, Henepola. *The Jhānas in Theravāda Buddhist Meditation*. The Wheel Publication, Sri Lanka, 1988.

Gunaratana, Henepola. The path of serenity and insight. Motilal Banarsidass Publishers, Delhi, 2016

Hampden-Turner, Charles. *Maps of the Mind*. McMillan, New York, 1982

Hendricks, Gay. *Conscious Living*. HarperCollins Publishers, San Francisco, 2000.

Henry, M, de Rivera, L, Gonzalez, I, Abreu, J. Improvement of respiratory function in chronic asthmatic patients with Autogenic Therapy. J. Psychosom. Res, 37:265-270 (1993).

Herrigel, Eugen. *Zen in the Art of Archery*. Vintage, New York, 1971

Hess, W. R. *The Biology of Mind.* The University of Chicago Press, Chicago, 1964.

Hess, W. R. *Diencephalon.* Grune & Stratton, New York, 1954.

Hofstadter, Douglas. I am a strange loop. Basic Books, New York, 2007

James, William. The Principles of Psychology. Holt, New York, 1890

Jaspers, Karl. *The Origin and Goal of History.* Routledge, Abingdon, 1953

Johnston, Charles. *Los Yoga Sutras de Patanjali.* Editorial Orion, México, 1975.

Kandel, Eric R., James H. Schwartz, Thomas M. Jessell. *Principles of Neural Science.*McGraw-Hill Companies, EE.UU., 2000.

Keenan, Sam. *Combining Kuhn and Jung: outlining a 'step ladder model' (SLM) for scientific discovery and paradigm shift research.* International Journal of Jungian Studies, 2015 Vol. 7: 1–21

LeDoux, Joseph, *Anxious,* Viking, New York, 2015

LeDoux, Joseph. *The Emotional Brain.* Simon and Schuster, new York, 1996

LeDoux, Joseph. *Synaptic Self,* Viking, New York, 2002

Luthe, Wolfgang. *The Clinical Significance of various forms of Autogenic Abreaction.* Proceedings of the Third World Congress of Psychiatry, University of Toronto

Press and McGill University Press, Montreal, 1961, vol. 3, pp. 485-488.

Luthe, Wolfgang. *Correlationes Psychomaticae.* Grune & Stratton, New York, 1965.

Luthe, Wolfgang. *Methods of Autogenic Therapy. An Introductory Workshop.* Create Space, Charleston, 2016.

Luthe, Wolfgang; Schultz, J. H. *Autogenic Therapy, Vol II: Medical Applications.* Grune & Stratton, New York, 1969.

Luthe, Wolfgang; Schultz, J. H. *Autogenic Therapy, Vol. III: Applications in Psychotherapy.* Grune & Stratton, New York, 1969.

Luthe, Wolfgang. *Autogenic Therapy, Vol IV: Research and Theory.* Grune & Stratton, New York, 1970.

Luthe, Wolfgang. *Autogenic Therapy, Vol.V: Dynamics of Autogenic Neutralization.* Grune & Stratton, New York, 1970.

Luthe, Wolfgang. *Autogenic Therapy, Vol. VI: Treatment with Autogenic Neutralization.* Grune & Stratton, New York, 1973.

Luthe, Wolfgang. The Creativity Mobilization Technique. Grune & Stratton, New York, 1976.

Luthe Wolfgang. *"Letres d'information sur les aspects neurofonctionnels de l'education".* Unpublished manuscript, Quebec 1975

MacLean, Paul D. *A triune concept of the brain and behaviour.* Toronto. University of Toronto Press, 1973

Marias, Julian. *Ataraxia y Alcionismo*, Instituto Ibys, Madrid, 1957

Masi, Luciano; Galli, Antonio. *Psicoterapia Autogena a Orientamento Analitico e Interpretazione Psicofisiologica.* CISU Centro d'Informazione e Stampa Universitaria di Colomartini Enzo, Roma, 2012.

Merton, Thomas. *Semillas de Contemplacion (Seeds of Comtemplation).* Editorial Sudamericana, Buenos Aires, 1952

Mishra, Rammurti S. *The Textbook of Yoga Psychology.* Julian Press, New York, 1971.

Naranjo, Claudio. *El carácter en la Relación de Ayuda.* Ediciones La Llave, Barcelona, 2015.

Naranjo, Claudio; Ornstein, Robert E. *On the Psychology of Meditation.* Viking Press, New York, 1971.

Nhat Hanh, Thihc. *Il miracolo della Presenza Mentale.* Ubaldini Editore, Roma, 1992.

Nikodimos, Saint and Makarios, Saint. *The Philokalia.* Faber and Faber, London, 1983.

Nussbaum, Martha C. *The Therapy of Desire.* Princeton University Press, New Jersey, 1994.

Palladino, Luciano. *Metodologie Autogene.* Edizioni ETImpresa, Torino, 2016.

Peirone, Luciano; Gerardi, Elena. *Il Training Autogeno.* Edizioni FerrariSinibaldi, Milano, 2016.

Penfield, Wilder. *The Mystery of the Mind.* Princeton University Press, New Jersey, 1975.

Penfield W and Rasmussen T. The cerebral cortex of man. By. The Macmillan Company, New York, N.Y. 1950. Pp. 248.

Penfield, Wilder and Roberts, Lamar. *Speech and Brain-Mechanisms.* Princeton University Press, New Jersey, 1959.

Ranty, Yves. *Le Training Autogène Progressif.* Presses Universitaires de France, Paris, 1990.

Royet Jean-Pierre Plailly Jane. Lateralization of Olfactory Processes. Chemical Senses, 2004, 29: 731–745

Ruiz, Miguel. *The Four Agreements.* Amber Allen, San Rafael, 1997.

Russell, Bertrand. *The Conquest of Happiness.* Liveright, London, 1930.

Sanchez-Gonzalez, Mikel. *The Primate Thalamus is a Key Target for Brain Dopamine. The Journal of Neuroscience,* 2005, 25: 6076–-6083

Scheler, Max. *Nature et Formes de la Sympathie.* Payot, Paris, 1950

Scheler, Max. *Formalism in Ethics and Non-Formal Ethics of Values.* Northwestern University Press, Evanston, 1973

Scholem, Gershom. Major Trends in Jewish Mysticism. New York, Schocken Books, 1974

Schultz, J. H. *Die seelische Krankenbehandlung.* Jena Verlag von Gustav Fischer, Germany, 1930.

Schultz JH: Oberstufe des autogenen Trainings und Raya-Yoga. Zeitschrift für die gesamte Neurologie und Psychiatrie 1932; 139: 1–34.

Schultz, J. H. *El entrenamiento autógeno.* Barcelona: Editorial Científico Medica, 1954.

Schultz, J. H. *Psicoterapia Bionomica.* Translated by Walter Orrù and Miranda Ottobre. Milano: Masson, 2001.

Schultz, J. H., and W. Luthe. *Autogenic Methods. Autogenic Therapy Vol. I.* New York: Grune & Stratton, 1969.

Selye, Hans. *The Physiology and Pathology of Exposure to Stress.* 1st ed. Montreal: Acta Medical Publishers, 1950.

Shafii, M. *Freedom from the Self. Sufism, Meditation and Psychotherapy.* New York: Human Sciences Press, 1985.

Shah, Idries. *The Sufis.* Doubleday, Newy York, 1971

Shannon, William H. *Thomas Merton's Dark Path.* The inner experience of a contemplative. Farrar-Straus-Giroux, New York, 1981

Sīlānanda, Sayadaw U. *The Four Foundations of Mindfulness.* Boston: Wisdom Publications, 2015.

Snyder, Stephen, and Tina Rasmussen. *Practicing the Jhānas.* Boulder, CO: Shambhala Publications, 2009.

Sogyal Rinpoche. The Tibetan Book of Living and Dying. London, Random House, 1992

Sperry Roger W., S. Gazzaniga Michael, and Joseph E. Bogen. "Interhemispheric Relationships: The Neocortical

Commissures; Syndromes of Hemisphere Disconnection." In *Handbook of Clinical Neurology*, edited by P. Vinken and G. Bruyn, 273–90. Amsterdam: North-Holland, 1969

Surya Das, Lama. *Awakening the Buddha Within*. New York: Broadway Book, 1997.

Tart, Charles T. *States of Consciousness*. New York: Dutton, 1975.

Trungpa, Chögyam. *Cutting Through Spiritual Materialism*. Boston: Shambhala, 1973.

Trungpa, Chögyam. *The Myth of the Freedom and the Way of Meditation*. Boston and Londres: Shambhala Library, 2005.

Trungpa, Chögyam. *Training the Mind*. Boston: Shambala Publications, 1993.

Wach-Ch'ug Dorje, the Ninth Karmapa. *The Mahāmudrā*. New Delhi: Library of Tibetan Works & Archives, 1978.

Wallace, Alan B. "The Buddhist Tradition of Samatha." *Journal of Consciousness Studies* 6, no. 2–3 (1999): 175–87.

Wallnöfer, Heinrich. *Auf der Suche nach dem Ich*. Stuttgart: Edition Hannemann, 1992.

Wallnöfer, Heinrich. *Sani con il Training Autogeno e la Psicoterapia Autogena*. Translated by Miranda Ottobre Gastaldo. Roma: Armando Editore, 2008.

Wallnöfer, Heinrich. *Seele ohne Angst*. Hamburg: Hoffmann und Campe Verlag, 1968.

Wassmann, Claudia. "Picturesque Incisiveness: Explaining the Celebrity of James's Theory of Emotion." *Journal of the History of the Behavioral Sciences* 50, no. 2 (Spring 2014): 166–88.

Watts, Alan W. *The Wisdom of Insecurity*. London: Rider and Company, 1976.

Widmann, Claudio. *Manuale di Training Autogeno e Tecniche di Psicoterapia Binomica*. Ravenna: Edizioni del Girasole, 2011.

Wong, Eva. *Seven Taoist Masters*. Boston: Shambala Publications, 1990.

NOTES

[1] In the early years of the millennium, Transcendental Meditation, made scientific by the Harvard Physician Herbert Benson, was going strong. A beautiful actress in full yoga posture anchored in the cover of *Time* magazine, the leading article of its August 4, 2003, issue, titled "The Science of Meditation." In the teens of the millennium, a second Harvard contribution, MBSR, for mindfulness-based stress reduction, took the lead, and an equally beautiful actress anchored the article "The Mindful Revolution" in the cover of *Time* magazine, February 3, 2014. If you would like to see the covers, just click

http://content.time.com/time/covers/0,16641,20030804,00.html.

http://content.time.com/time/subscriber/article/0,33009,2163560,00.html.

[2] Sayadaw U. Silananda gives in *The Four Foundations of Mindfulness* what is probably the most accurate and useful rendering of the *Maha Satipatthan Sutta*, The Great Discourse on the Foundations of Mindfulness.

[3] See Wallace 1999 in bibliography. *Samatha* is a state in which it is easy to maintain total, steady, unwavering, and clear concentration.

[4] For a more complete account of this history, see de Rivera, *Psicoterapia Autogena*, segunda edicion (Madrid: ICAT Information Center, 2017). There is an Italian translation: de Rivera, *Psicoterapia Autogena* (Cortina, Torino, 2009).

[5] Luthe, "Autogenic Abreaction," in *Autogenic Therapy* vol. VI.

[6] See de Rivera, "Autogenic Abreaction and Psychoanalysis" and "Autogenic Analysis: The Tool Freud Was Looking for."

[7] de Rivera, "Drugs, States of Consciousness and Creativity" and "the Circular Dynamics of Drug Addiction."

[8] Naranjo and Ornstein, *On the Psychology of Meditation*. He signed my copy with these words: "To Luis, seeker, psychoanalyst and great person, wishing him always new horizons." I took it as a mandate.

[9] Benson, *The Relaxation Response*. He mentions autogenic training among the methods to induce the relaxation response. Benson studied a large number of disciples of Maharishi Mahesh Yogi during the practice of Transcendental Meditation. His close relationship with Maharishi broke later on, and he became an advocate of meditation as a science, as opposed to meditation as a religious movement or, worse, a profitable business.

[10] de Rivera, "La spécialisation hémisphérique et les états de conscience," Revue Française de Relaxation Psychothérapique, 1997, 18:81-98.

[11] Luis de Rivera and Reyes Trujillo. Paroxistic discharges and microabreactions of traumatic events are probably more frequent in autogenics, due to the specific effects of dual concentration in the enhancement of interhemispheric communication. Nevertheless, they also occur in other meditation methods, although they are rarely acknowledged, probably because the lack of an appropriate theory to explain those phenomena and of a proper method to handle them.

[12] Luis de Rivera, Reyes Trujillo, Alberto Chiessa, Yves Ranty, Giovanni Gastaldo, Miranda Ottobre, Manuel Abuin, and Concha Gomez-Cantero met in Luzern, Switzerland, from 15 to 19 June 2010, and participated in the Symposium ASCI Therapies, the twentieth World Congress of International Federation for Psychotherapy.

[13] William James, "The Stream of Consciousness," in *The Principles of Psychology*, vol. I, 224–90.

[14] There are many good reviews of the history of meditation, such as those by LeShan, Goleman, Eliade, and James. My forthcoming book *The Many Ways of Meditation* elaborates on the common ground and the many variants of the consciousness-training procedures, including spontaneous developments.

[15] Sam Keenan (see bib.) studies many reports of creative scientist who had the first glimpses of their theories in dreams or in altered states of consciousness. See also my article Creativity and Psychosis in Scientific Research.

[16]The original yoga sutras of Patanjali are a very short text written in Sanskrit. There is discussion among the scholars as to its exact

timing, which has been variously calculated between 200 BC and 400 AD. Translation and commentaries written in 1917 by Johnston, *The Yoga Sutras of Patanjali: The Book of the Spiritual Man*. The edition I have is in Spanish by Editorial Orion, Mexico, 1975. Also see Rammurti S. Mishra, The Textbook of Yoga Psychology, The Julian Press, New York, 1963.A complete list of the sutras can be found in the link http://www.swamij.com/yoga-sutras-list.htm

[17]*The Visuddhimagga*, in English The Path of Purification, was written in Pali, the language spoken by Buddha, in AD 500. It is considered the most authoritative rendering of the Theravada tradition. It compiles and comments the Pali Canon, collection of old scriptures known as the Tipitaka because they were stored in three baskets (*pitakas*): The Vinaya, containing instructions for the monastic life, the Suttas, collection of Buddha discourses, and the Abhidhamma, psycho-philosophical elaborations of the Suttas.

[18] Of the myriad of texts introducing Buddhism to the occidentals, my favorite, because of its high ratio *Learning/Difficulty,* is the one by the American Lama Sunya Das. All religions and mystical schools have a triple base formed by theoretical considerations, norms of conduct, and a meditative technique.

[19] One of the ways of Zen is meditation in action, doing something in a precise manner, with full concentration on what you are doing. Zen and the Art of Archery recounts the famous experience of Eugen Herrigel with his Japanese master. Less known and also based in Zen principles is Gallwey's The Inner Game of Tennis, which greatly improved my game. In fact, the Zen mentality may be applied to any activity, from flower arrangement (Ikebana, in Japanese) to the tea ceremony or, simply, to walking.

[20] Karl Jaspers, a German psychiatrist and philosopher of the XX century, described in his book *The Origin and Goal of History* what he called "the time axis of history", short periods of extraordinary socio-cultural change, interspersed among long dull periods in which nothing particularly interesting happens.

[21] The three main schools of Hellenistic philosophy were the Stoics, the Epicureans and the Skeptics. The best treatise I know about their efforts to construct a Therapeutic Philosophy and achieve happiness

through reasoning is by Martha C. Nussbaum, The Therapy of Desire. Theory and Practice of Hellenistic Ethics. Princeton University Press, New Jersey, 1994. Other worthy books are *Art of living* by Epictetus and the short essay by Julian Marias, *Ataraxia y Alcionismo*, Instituto Ibys, Madrid, 1957

[22] It is difficult to find in the Jewish Mystical literature instructions to induce special states of consciousness, or even poetic renderings of such states. This is a big difference with meditative practices in other cultures. It seems to me that the seekers of this tradition are more interested in the objective description of God and Its attributes than in transmitting the inner experience and the path to attain it. For an overview of Jewish Mysticism, see Scholem excellent treatise. Baigent and Leigh offer an interesting, albeit controversial, view on the Essenian contribution to Christianism.

[23] Saint Nikodimos of the Holy Mountain and Saint Makarios of Corinth were the main compilers of The Philokalia. Interspersed with its many pious and ascetic considerations, there is much practical advice to get to the Presence of God through mental training in praying.

[24] The Pray of the Heart is a practice well known to orthodox Christians, recovered in the west by some neo-charismatic Catholics. The version I like the best consists in imagining the face of Christ in the own heart and repeating mentally a short prayer. See the Philokalia and the Way of the Pilgrim.

[25] Saint Teresa de Jesus, the great mystic nun of 1550 Spain, describes in her *Castillo Interior*, The Interior Castle, seven *Moradas* or dwellings that sound powerfully similar to the samadhi experience in the Jhanas. Lance Cousins has published a relevant chapter on this coincidence in the book on comparative mysticism edited by Karel Werner. Those comparative studies of different meditation procedures are a very important for the study of mindfulness, because they confirm the existence of a human capacity that can be developed by different methods or even spontaneously.

[26] Thomas Merton is a last century exponent of the "apophatic tradition", also called *via negativa* or the dark path, because it seeks the contemplation of God not through His attributes, but through

what He is not. Older exponents of this Christian contemplative tradition are Saint Juan de la Cruz, Master Eckhart, and the unknown author of the medieval mystical treatise The Cloud of Unknowing. Merton's advice: "open yourself to your inner truth and to grace and contemplation may enter your life unobserved"

[27] Tony de Mello was born in India, professed as a Jesuit in Spain, studied psychology in USA and worked as a psychotherapist. His eclectic approach, combining the Spiritual Exercises of St. Ignatius of Loyola with Hindu and Buddhist traditions, was not fully approved by the Vatican.

[28] Idries Shah is the main exponent of Sufism in occident. Albeit his descriptions are more literary than technical, he transmits what we could call the "Sufi attitude". More practical is treatise on Sufi meditation applied to psychotherapy by Shafii (Freedom from the Self, Human Sciences Press, New York)

[29] Weekend courses in "Mindfulness" and other simplified demos for business executives are gaining surprising acclaim, much to the dismay of the traditional serious teachers. Purser and Loy are dubbing this popular trend "McMindfulness", in allusion to the successful commercialization of cheap junk food. Accepting that the banalization of meditation has its risks, it also opens the interest for this field to the general public, and should open it to serious professionals as well. No doctor, specially psychiatrists and clinical psychologists, can afford today to ignore the scientific basis of meditation, its many benefits for health and the adverse reactions produced by careless practice.

[30] Chögyam Trungpa says in his book Cutting Through Spiritual Materialim:. "it is not a matter of building up the awakened state of mind, but rather of burning out the confusions which obstruct it. In the process of burning out these confusions, we discover enlightenment. If the process were otherwise, the awakened state of mind would be a product, dependent upon cause and effect and therefore liable to dissolution. Anything which is created must, sooner or later, die. If enlightenment were created in such a way, that there would always be the possibility of ego reasserting itself, causing a return to the confused state. Enlightenment is permanent because we have not produced it; we have merely discovered it. In

the Buddhist tradition the analogy of the sun appearing from behind the clouds is often used to explain the discovery of enlightenment."

[31] The Way begins anew with each new master. The Way is not really a tradition but a Principle, to be developed by each master in his own personal manner.

[32] George Ivanovitch Gurdjieff was a mysterious man, of whose origins and teachers little is known. He was born in the Caucasus-Kurdistan frontier and stablished himself in Moscu around 1910. His fame attracted the journalist Piotr Demiánovich Ouspenski, who became his most famous and prolific pupil. They left Russia after the revolution and stablished schools in Constantinople, London and Paris. Gurdjieff's school is a very personal integration of Muslim, Orthodox and Hindu approaches.

[33] Beyond resilience – the capacity to stand trauma without deterioration – is the development of immunity to trauma through personal growth. My study of healthy persons who had surpassed severe crises reveals that their posttraumatic growth follows a sequence of seven psychological steps: Centering – Keeping calm – Minimizing harm – Understanding the situation – Deciding the condition – Becoming a proactive person – Evolving. See *Crisis Emocionales, pp 173-188.* The systematic application of this natural psychological evolution to eclectic psychotherapy has allowed me to create the method *PSI - Psicoterapia secuencial integradora –* Integrative Sequential Psychotherapy – see *Sindromes de Estrés.* pp. 249-260

[34] There are several words in German translated as understanding. *Verstehen* relates to our understanding of others. *Erlebnis*, by itself does not provide self-understanding. Self-understanding is obtained to the extent that the self relates to itself as it relates to others, i.e., in a mediated way. *Erlebnis* remains the psychological source of all experience, the experiential potential that is articulated and conceptualized in understanding. Jhon Arthos (see "To Be Alive When Something Happens: Retrieving Dilthey's Erlebnis") gives a clarifying, albeit heavily philosophical, description of *Erlebnis*, but fails to find a precise English word for it. Ortega y Gasset translated *Erlebnis* to Spanish as *Vivencia* and made it a cornerstone of his philosophy. In *Crisis Emocionales* (pp. 82 and 83) I discuss the

practical distinction between event (*acontecimiento*) experience (*experience*) and live-experience (*vivencia*).

[35] This memory is taken from my essay "The journey as a generator of creative crises." Being immersed in a culture where the strangest things are taken as fully normal changes your mind. Avoid people from your culture when you are abroad, mix with the natives. See *Crisis Emocionales*, pp. 122-124

[36] There is a hilarious Spanish film, "Why do they say love when they mean sex?" In fact, the sexual experience is only one of the four kinds of interactive love, also called sharing love.

[37] I am not referring to the conditional, wavering, weak, provisional decisions we make every day, but to the unshakable compromise with oneself that Castañeda calls unbending intent and *Sogyal Rimpoche Ngé jung* inTibetan. See notes 68 and 69

[38] Wallace, B.A.: The Buddhist Tradition of Samatha. (Journal of Consciousness Studies, 1999, 6:175-187) is an excellent scholarly clarification of this essential concept, so hard to translate (and to understand) in western languages.

[39] The TABS (Tenerife Autogenic Brain Scan) project was possible by a grant from the University of La Laguna in Canarias and the generous participation of 15 experienced volunteers, most of them autogenic therapist. The project was presented at the III World Congress of Science and Meditation in 2015 and published in the International Journal of Autogenic Research

[40] This sea hare is an excellent subject for neurobiological studies, because his big neurons are easy to isolate and stimulate. Eric Kandel won the Nobel Prize in Medicine experimenting with Aplysias.

[41] Luis de Rivera, Psiconeuroendocrinolgia, Inteva, Madrid, 1981, pp. 6

[42] MacLean continued the studies of Papez on the limbic system and his anatomical contributions are very important and widely recognized. However, his Triune Brain Theory includes some phylogenetic considerations that are not so well accepted and not fully corroborated by research.

[43] In fact, Hess description was concerned with structures of the diencephalon, although he identified some hypothalamic connections to the cortex, the limbic system and all over the body through the sympathetic and parasympathetic branches of the autonomic nervous system.

[44]MacLean's Triune Brain Theory makes a lot of intuitive sense and provides a neurobiological basis to the classic metaphor of the human mind as a chariot: The horses are the passions –limbic system-, the driver is the reason – the cortex - and the chariot the body – the diencephalon.

[45] *Crisis Emocionales*, pag 161. Previously published in JLG de Rivera, A. Vela and J. Arana (Eds.), *Manual de Psiquiatria*, Karpos, Madrid, pag. 747

[46] See in bibliography Hess, Luthe, Gellhorn, Roland Fisher.

[47] Selye does not mention Cannon in his early works, although they were both studying the same endocrine organ, the suprarenal or adrenal gland. Only, Selye was interested in the cortical part of the gland, which produces cortisone and other corticoids, and Cannon in the inner part, the adrenal medulla, which produces adrenaline and noradrenaline. Selye made famous the word "stress"

[48] Cannon was a pioneer of physiology on the early XX century and discover, among many other things, the mechanisms of the hypovolemic shock, of the "Voodoo Death" and of arterial hypertension. Even if he is a pioneer in the study of stress, he did not use the word at all in his publications. He quoted the pioneer experiments of Gregorio Marañon demonstrating the Cognitive-Visceral theory of emotion, an antecedent ignored by the official proponents of this theory, Singer and Sachter.

[49] Herbert Benson was the first MD who cared about the physiology of meditation and published the scientific studies that made the technique respectable. He had a busy practice in the Beth Israel Hospital in New York and became a celebrity in the mid-seventies. He teamed for a time with Maharishi Mahesh Yogi, the introducer of Transcendental Meditation (TM) in the USA, but later disagreed with he considered a mercantilist and sectarian approach, especially after Maharishi registered TM as trade mark.

[50] Heinrich Wallnöfer, *Seele ohne Angst, pp. 63-64*

[51] Ruth Feldman. The Neurobiology of Human Attachment. TICS, https://www.researchgate.net/publication/311971636_The_Neurobiology_of_Human_Attachments

[52] Great revision of the relation hypothalamus-hypophysis by Lechan RM, Toni R. Functional Anatomy of the Hypothalamus and Pituitary. [Updated 2016 Nov 28]. In: De Groot LJ, Chrousos G, Dungan K, et al., editors. Endotext [Internet]. South Dartmouth (MA): MDText.com, Inc.; 2000-Available from: https://www.ncbi.nlm.nih.gov/books/NBK279126/

[53] In 1978 my General Law of Homeostasis was awarded the Silver Medal of the Royal Society of Medicine of Spain. It was published afterwards it in my books *Medicina Psicosomatica* and S*indromes de Estrés*. A short summary is in my paper *Homeostasis, Allostasis and Adaptation.* The basic idea is that each physiological and biochemical variable has an optimal value which corresponds to maximum health, vitality and longevity. Variations from this optimal value can be tolerated by the organism for a time, specific for each variable. In mathematical terms, health is maintained if the quotient $(N + \text{variation of } N)*T / Rg+Ra$ is lower than 1. Being N = the variable, T = the length of time the value of this variable deviates from its optimal value, Rg = the genetic resistance (or tolerance) of the organism to variations of this variable from the optimal value and Ra = the acquired tolerance. For instance, the tolerance to variations of the blood pH is very small, and severe illness will develop in seconds with a change of only 0,6 % of the optimal value. By contrast, cholesterol blood levels can be elevated three fold for years, without any apparent disturbance. The psychological version of the General Law of Homeostasis is in *Crisis Emocionales,* chapter 5, *El sindrome de la rana cocida* – The cooked frog syndrome, pp.103-124

[54] You may think fighting and flying are opposing activities, but for your hypothalamus they are basically the same. It is the limbic system who knows the difference, because fight comes with anger and flying with fear.

[55] It is well known that the autogenic state lasts for some time after finishing the basic exercises. The feeling of relaxation persists for about an hour, whereas the increased perception and the autogenic

discharges are inhibited by the standard termination procedure. While experimenting with the partial exercises, I came to the discovery that merely remembering the calm body sensations right after terminating the basic exercises would bring back the feeling of relaxation, so I described in 1999 the "Memory exercise", *Ejercicio del recuerdo*, see my Psicoterapia Autogena, 1999, p. 84. The closer to termination this exercise is performed, the easier is the access to the somatic memory of relaxation. Trainees are taught to perform the memory exercise a few minutes after termination at first, and then practice it at progressively longer intervals. The memory exercise can be done at fixed times (i.e. every hour), at moments of need (stressful situations) or can be paired with an external stimulus (conditioning of the relaxation response). The memory exercise and the conditioning of the relaxation response are also described in my Entrenamiento Autogeno, 2015, pp. 106 and 107.

[56] The reticular formation is a network of neurons throughout the brain stem that connects the motor (descending pathway) and the sensory nerves (ascending pathway) to and from the spinal cord, cerebellum, and cerebrum. It was first described by Moruzzi and Magoun in 1949 who found that its activation arouses the cerebral cortex. Routtenberg (1968) demonstrated that this system maintains the arousal level of the organism. https://en.wikiversity.org/wiki/Motivation_and_emotion/Book/2014/Reticular_formation,_arousal_and_emotion

[57] Joseph LeDoux discovered the role of the amygdala in the non-conscious aspects of fear, and his findings are compatible with my theory that limbic processing transforms the physical activation of the autonomic nervous system in subjective opinions (feelings), which are further processed by the cognitive systems in the neocortex. There are, however, many shortcuts, that on occasions may be life-saving. There is such a wealth of internal connections in the brain that the three systems may function in parallel, at the same time that they do it in sequential processes.

[58] Luis de Rivera, *Sindromes de Estres. La Biologia de las Emociones.* pp. 61-74

[59] De Rivera, L, Gonzalez-Mora, JL, Hernandez Martin, E. et al: Brain activation by Autogenic training. A fMRI study. International Journal of Autogenic Research, in press.

[60] In fact, while most of the fibers of the olfactory nerve are ipsilateral, there is a small number that go to the contralateral hemisphere via the anterior commissure. The cognitive processing of smells differs in both hemispheres, with the right hemisphere involved in memory processes and the left hemisphere in emotional processes. (see Royet and Plailly, 2004)

[61] The differences in cognitive specialization of the two sides of the brain were known since Paul Broca discovered the location of the speech area in 1861 and further explored by Wilder Penfield in the early 1950, but it was in the late sixties when Roger Sperry, Michael Gazzaniga, and Joseph Bogen made their definitive contribution by their psychological experiments on fully functional split-brain subjects.

[62] Figures taken from Penfield's book *Speech Mechanisms.* Dominant hemisphere, p. 200. Nondominant hemisphere, p. 214.

[63] Blausen.com, Medical Gallery of Blausen Medical 2014. WikiJournal of Medicine 1 (2). DOI:10.15347/wjm/2014.010. ISSN 2002-4436. https://commons.wikimedia.org/w/index.php?curid=31574257

[64] The cerebral cortex of man. By Wilder Penfield and Theodore Rasmussen. The Macmillan Company, New York, N.Y. 1950. 248

[65] Luthe W *"Letres d'information sur les aspects neurofonctionnels de l'education"* is an unpublished manuscript he prepeared for his course at the *Centre de Développement en Environnement Scolaire de l'Université du Quebec* from september 1975 to february 1976

[66] Luthe's theory of interhemispheric disconnection produced by incompatible or contradictory information will be discussed at length in the last chapter of this book.

[67] Stephen Snyder and Tina Rasmussen present an easy introduction in their book*: Practicing the Jhanas: Traditional Concentration Meditation as Presented by the Venerable Pa Auk Sayadaw* . More scholarly is Gunaratana, simplified and divulgated by Goleman.

[68] Energic and immovable decision, *Ngé jung* in Tibetan Buddhism, literally "definite emergence" consists in total renouncing of distractions, not having the slightest interest for anything that gets in the way of liberation. *Sogyal Rimpoche. The Tibetan Book of Living and Dying*

[69] Unbending intent is an "Extremely well defined purpose not countermanded by any conflicting interests or desires" *Carlos Castañeda, The Power of Silence*

[70] Pat Cowings has been training astronauts for the NASA for over 40 years and is a pioneer on the combination of Autogenic Training and Biofeedback. She first presented her work in Rome in the World Congress of Psychosomatic Medicine in 1975 and her first papers were published in W. Luthe and F. Antonelly (Eds,) Autogenic Therapy, Roma, Edizioni Luigi Pozzi, Roma 1977

[71] There is some discussion on whether the autogenic formulas should contain the possessive determiner "my". Vedantic minded masters argue that, if the final purpose of meditation is transcending the ego and achieving the final dissolution of the self in nirvana, the use of pronouns and possessive determiners would retard this process. My point is that, to transcend the ego, you need first to have an ego and take full contact and possession of it. Autogenics begins by owning your body, continues by owning your feelings, then by owning the cognitive processes of your internal world and finally by owning your position in the universe. Once you achieve all this, you may worry about nirvana and dissolving the ego.

[72] Luthe recommends this formula in his Introductory Workshops to Autogenic Methods, but never introduced it formally among the six basic standard exercises of Autogenics 1.0

[73] The Many Ways of Mindfulness, soon to come.

[74] Magda Arnold is an important exception. And lately Damasio as well.

[75] It is customary in all texts on psychotherapy to affirm that it is necessary to be in "touch with your feelings", "aware of your feelings", "accept your feelings", and none explains how to do it, with the important exception of Gay Hendricks, who used "feeling the feeling" before me. The expression "Feeling the feeling" was also used by the phenomenologist Max Scheler, Feeling (verb) is a

mental function of perception and feeling (noun) is the content to be perceived. Hence, feeling the feeling requires maintaining steady perception of a live-experience, regardless of how pleasant or unpleasant it is. It means concentrating all energies in the perception process, avoiding all action, mental or physical.

[76] Unless we accept the possibility of "unconscious opinions". The diencephalon is making this kind of opinions all the time. For instance, the hypothalamus may detect blood sugar levels lower than those necessary for the appropriate nourishing of the cell, then activate the ergotropic system and get your body moving to the fridge.

[77] The amygdala has direct connections to the motor areas and to the striatum, which may facilitate a motor response to a threat before a feeling could be formed through the cingulate pathway and much before the cortex could organize a reasonable response to the situation. LeDoux, J.E. (2000). Emotion circuits in the brain. Annu. Rev. Neurosci. *23*, 155–184. This explains the startle reaction and the immediate release of the motor components of the fight and flight response. Training in feeling meditation enhances the performance of the cingulate pathway in the limbic system and reduces that of the extra-limbic connections of the amygdala.

[78] A new pathway from the limbic system and the hypothalamus, the thalamic dopaminergic system, has been discovered recently by my colleague Mikel Sanchez-Gonzalez (J. of Neuroscience, 2005). This fifth pathway adds to the four well known nigrostriatal, mesolimbic, mesocortical and tubero-infundibular dopaminergic pathways.

[79] William James is the name that comes to mind when asked about the scientific study of emotion, but his theories are far outmoded. See Claudia Wassmann article Picturesque incisiveness: explaining the celebrity of James's theory of emotion. *Journal of the History of the Behavioral Sciences*, Vol. 50(2), 166–188 Spring 2014. See also the paper What is emotion, by Michel Cabanac

[80] There are three types of adaptation: Alloplastic (changing the environment to adapt to you), Autoplastic (changing yourself to fit in the environment) and Heteroplastic (moving to a better place). See my paper *Homeostasis, Allostasis and Adaptation*.

[81] Life is in the diencephalon; the limbic system decides what to do with your life and the cortex finds out how to do it.

[82] Luthe observed that crying discharges are frequent during the autogenic state, and that the interruption of the exercise at this point left the patient with a lasting experience of discomfort. When the crying discharges are blocked or resisted during the exercise, concentration becomes difficult and there is frequent apparition of headaches or other somatic symptoms. Forced crying was the first neutralization technique invented by Luthe, to facilitate the acceptance of crying and the disposal of the chronic resistance to crying developed by education. Crying has a beneficial psycho-physiological effect, allowing the conversion of unbearable feelings to a complex muscular-visceral response. It also has a psycho-social function, signaling to the bystanders the pain the crying person is suffering. Both aspects have evolutive value, the first because crying is probably the only mind-body conversion pathway that in not harmful, and the second because it signals the distress of the infant and small child to the caregivers. But as the child grows up, he is taught and trained to inhibit crying, and the anti-homeostatic learned reflex of crying-inhibition is learned. All the mechanisms involved in crying are subject to conscious control, except the lacrimal glands. Forced crying seeks to re-start the crying mechanisms to its natural functioning, undoing the learned inhibition of crying.

[83] When I was experimenting with feeling meditation, I was quite concerned with suffering. In fact, I was not meditating on feelings, but on suffering. I came to an elaborate theory I called the "Zero point". I imagined suffering increased until it got to a point from where it could not get any worse. This was the Zero Point. From there, there was no furthered sinking into despair. At the Zero Point, I could either disappear or keep existing. Then, the sense of existence came to me, and I realized that only progress could be made from there, this is why I called the experience the Zero Point. After trying the experience of the Zero Point several times, I realized that it was unnecessary. What I thought was the deepest possible suffering was, in reality, the extreme evolution of despair. And after allowing the feeling of despair coming to the end, the feeling of hope appears just by itself. I understood the meaning of

"While there is life there is hope". If the only feeling left is the feeling of existence, you come to the first certitude "I exist" – See my Prologue to Claudio Naranjo's book on Enneatypes and transference.

[84] With the significant exception of Gay Hendricks´ excellent book "Conscious living".

[85] The Satipathana says "concentrating on the feelings as feelings," which, according to me, means the same as "feeling the feeling" and is not thinking, understanding, discussing, acting or anything else.

[86] Luthe's vols. V and VI of his series on Autogenic Therapy: - Dynamics of Autogenic neutralization (vol V) and treatment with Autogenic abreaction (vol. VI)

[87] The ideoplastic principle is an extension of the ideomotor principle and is basic to the Autogenic Modification Methods. See de Rivera, *Psicoterapia Autogena*

[88] Adapting is not a sign of resigned conforming. There are three kinds of adaptation: Autoplastic adaptation, transforming oneself to fit in the environment, like developing muscles to lift weights, Alloplastic adaptation, transforming the environment to our convenience, like building a house, and heteroplastic adaptation, moving to another environment where the two other types of adaptation are expected to be unnecessary or at least easier

[89] The first Noble Truth of Buddha is *"life is duhkka"* The Pali word *duhkka* is difficult to translate, and has been variously rendered as suffering, fastidious, hard, difficult, anxiety, distress, frustration, unease, un-satisfactoriness. Many translators prefer to leave it untranslated. The second Truth is "the cause of suffering is attachment to impermanent things, that cannot be satisfying because they are transitory" It would be better to say that the cause of dukkha is the ignorance of the impermanence. The third Truth is "There is a way out of ignorance" and the fourth Truth ends by a magnificent marketing pitch "The way out of ignorance is the Eightfold Way" (Buddha's method)

[90] See the great musical Singing in the Rain. Besides entertaining yourself, you will learn how to go from despairing failure to happy success, at least in the movies.

[91] There is so much information, from clinical studies to genetic research, that reviewing it would take a full book. A scientific study of traditional practices of very old healthy people is the study of Todd Pesek, MD, Ronald Reminick, PhD, and Murali Nair, PhD: Secrets of long life: cross-cultural explorations in sustainably enhancing vitality and promoting longevity via elders' practice wisdom. Explore 2010; 6:352-358.

[92] *The Jhanas in Theravada Buddhist Meditation*, by Mahathera Henepola Gunaratana.

[93] Attachment to suffering is a common pitfall in some forms of religious meditation. Passive acceptance of suffering is not the same that attachment to suffering. In fact, they are practically the contrary. A serious technical error in feeling meditation is giving importance to suffering. (See note 83).

[94] See *Crisis Emocionales*. The ideograms of Chinese language allow forms of thinking difficult to achieve with our words.

[95] TonGlen consists on meditating on evil without aversion nor desire, taking in all that is bad and giving out all that is good. It may seem to be the ultimate on feeling transmutation, but it has to be done with outmost caution and under the personal care of a very experienced master. There is a point when you become extra sensitive to pain and suffering. Your usual armor has been slowly dissolving by meditation, and you see suffering as it appears to be at first sight: horrible. It happened to me with the death of a toreador in Spain and the joy expressed by the anti-taurine in the social media. I felt the pain of the bull, and I could stand it. I felt the pain of the dying torero and the pain of his family, and I could stand it. Then I felt the joy of the anti-taurine at the death of the torero, and I could not stand it. Something broke in my world; nothing seemed to make sense any longer. If suffering for the suffering of an animal is evidence of your empathy with life and of your *bodhisattva* attitude, how can this be compatible with the joy for the suffering and death of a human? I happened to be at lunch with Claudio Naranjo at this time, and, as I was explaining my difficulty, he said "you must first decide what is more important, the life of the torero or the life of the bull". I took the answer at face value, I remembered something from Hofstadter about how to measure consciousness in units he called

"hunekes", but, before I could say anything, they all started to laugh and the topic was dropped. They were not taking me seriously. I was left looking for a vegetarian to ask him what is more important, the life of a lamb or the life of an artichoke.

[96] I am indebted to the Aikidoka Dr. Tomas Gomez Mena for teaching me those basic principles of Aikido.

[97] Let us avoid the old discussion about the relationship between the brain and the mind, which probably is an unanswerable question. Wilder Penfield, the great brain explorer, was convinced of the existence of an independent mind, "a quantum of energy who activates brain areas as I do with my scalpel" he told me when he was writing his "Mystery of the Mind", shortly before his death. By contrast, Wolfgang Luthe, the great explorer of consciousness, was a firm believer that all human experience boiled down to nervous connections. Both were convinced of their personal truths beyond the need of any reasonable proof; both tended to get irritated if contradicted, a telltale sign that marks the difference between science and belief. I tell my anecdotes with them in my paper "Structure and function of the Human Mind."

[98] See my papers on creativity, specially Creativity and Psychosis and *Estados de Consciencia y Creatividad*

[99] This lexical problem does not exist in Italian, giving better rein to talk about *auto-coscienza*, which means self-awareness, albeit the literal translation would be self-consciousness. In the 2014 meeting of ECAAT-CISSPAT in Padova I had the opportunity to discuss the role of *auto-coscienza* in the evolution of the universe, an idea I got from reading Teilhard de Chardin in my adolescence.

[100] Hampden-Turner's 1982 book graphically reviews 60 concepts of mind, from antiquity to the mid-seventies. Unfortunately, he missed the meditative-psychedelic wave, that launched precisely when his book ends.

[101] Naming something facilitates understanding, yet the name creates boundaries that separate the thing named from the rest of the related experience. Maps and images do a little bit better in terms of continuity and contextually. Yet, the map is not the territory; it may help, but does not substitute the live-experience.

[102] There is some confusion with this concept. Authenticity is not doing what first comes to mind, or what you feel like, or being inconsiderate to others. Authenticity is being free from automatisms, acting out of the inner core of the self without fear nor desire, doing what is right for you and for the situation.

[103] See my bibliography on creativity. All in Spanish, *creatividad*, except one paper in French in the *Revue Française de Relaxation Psychotherapique.*

TERM AND NAME INDEX

This index of terms and names is far from exhaustive. Its simple purpose is to supplement the Table of Contents and facilitate the localization of some key autogenic concepts in the book.

CPSIA information can be obtained
at www.ICGtesting.com
Printed in the USA
BVHW031813090419
545073BV00001B/28/P